A Guide for Change

Resources for Implementing Community Service Writing

1996

A GUIDE FOR CHANGE

Resources for Implementing
Community Service Writing

Ann Watters
Stanford University

Marjorie Ford
Stanford University

1995

McGRAW-HILL, INC.

New York   St. Louis   San Francisco   Auckland
Bogotá   Caracas   Lisbon   London   Madrid   Mexico City   Milan
Montreal   New Delhi   San Juan   Singapore   Sydney   Tokyo   Toronto

This book was set in Palatino by Ann Eisner.
The editors were Tim Julet and Scott Amerman;
the production supervisor was Paula Keller.
The cover was designed by Raphael Hernandez.
R. R. Donnelley & Sons Company was printer and binder.

A GUIDE FOR CHANGE
Resources for Implementing Community Service Writing

This book is printed on recycled, acid-free paper, containing 10% postconsumer waste.

1 2 3 4 5 6 7 8 9 0 DOC DOC 9 0 9 8 7 6 5 4

ISBN 0-07-068617-3

About the Authors

ANN WATTERS is a lecturer in English at Stanford University. She has directed the Program in Writing and Critical Thinking at Stanford and co-developed and co-directed the Community Service Writing Project. She has co-authored *Coming from Home* (1993) with Marjorie and Jon Ford and *Creating America: Reading and Writing Arguments* (1995) with Joyce Penn Moser. She also authored a forthcoming interactive CD-ROM multimedia program for teaching rhetoric.

MARJORIE FORD is a lecturer in English at Stanford University where she teaches in the Program in Writing and Critical Thinking and edits the program's newsletter, *Notes in the Margins*. With Jon Ford she has co-authored and edited *Dreams and Inward Journeys* (1990 and 1994), *Writing as Revelation* (1992), and *Imagining Worlds* (1995). With Jon Ford and Ann Watters she has co-authored and edited *Coming from Home* (1993).

Writing for Change: A Community Reader and *A Guide for Change: Resources for Implementing Community Service Writing* were developed out of their experiences working in the Community Service Writing Project, which is jointly run by the Writing and Critical Thinking Program and the Haas Center for Public Service at Stanford University.

Contents

Preface

A *Guide for Change* is designed to help students develop writing for audiences not only within and beyond the classroom and college walls. Whether such writing takes the form of editorials and essays for the local newspapers, reflective essays and journals on student community service, or writing on behalf of community groups and organizations, we hope that the materials that follow will help guide students to become writers in the worlds both within and beyond the academy.

A Guide for Change is designed for instructors and students who would like to consider ways to integrate real-world writing or community work into their courses, particularly writing courses. We suggest ways to integrate community service writing into courses in a limited way—a letter to the editor as a substitute for one short essay, for example—or in a more prominent role—a research paper on a topic of community interest that is submitted to a local government or community agency. Yet a third way to integrate community service writing is to enable students to compose articles, proposals, informational brochures, or some other type of writing for local community groups and to submit such work for one or more of their course assignments. Since community service writing on behalf of local community groups is a newer approach for a composition course, we have offered the most guidance on this specific type of assignment.

We believe that several important goals are accomplished through community service writing. Such writing helps develop audience awareness, since students write not only for an audience of peers and an instructor but also for interested readers outside the classroom, giving student writers a real stake in writing not only to get a grade, but to communicate information and ideas.

Community service writing also gives students more investment in their learning and provides opportunities for them to reflect critically on their efforts and on important social and community issues. And in many respects, community service writing links student writers to the ancient roots of the discipline of rhetoric, encouraging them to take a public stand on important issues.

In undertaking a project of this nature, we relied on the guidance and support of many colleagues and friends. First of all, we thank our colleagues at the Haas Center for Public Service and elsewhere in the University, notably Tim Stanton, Janet Luce, Don Kennedy, Tom Wasow, Al Camarillo, Carolyn Lougee, Jeremy Cohen, and Shirley Brice Heath. We particularly thank our students whose diligence and engagement in writing and in their communities have provided the impetus for this project; their efforts and creativity form the core of this text. We thank our colleagues in our own department and at institutions around the country, especially Susan Wyle, Richard Holeton, Carolyn Ross, Carolyn Keen, Kay Butler-Nalin at University of Northern Iowa, Patricia O'Connor at Georgetown University, Joyce Speiller-Morris at University of Miami, Edward Zlotkowski at Bentley College, and our colleagues at Campus Compact and the Johnson Foundation, who have offered encouragement, advice, and unfailing support and constructive criticism. We offer special thanks to the following reviewers: Ken Autrey, Francis Marion College; Michael Berberich, Galveston College; Susan Brown Carlton, Pacific Lutheran University; Liz Buckley, East Texas State University; Robin Calitri, Merced College; Walter Cannon, Central College; Michael Cochran, Santa Fe Community College; Kirk Combe, Denison University; David Crowner, Gettysburg College; Betty Dixon, Rancho Santiago Community College; Paul Doherty, Boston College; Pat Donahue, Lafayette College; Susann Dorman, Louisiana State University; Wade Dorman, Louisiana State University; Cathy Fleischer, Eastern Michigan University; Susan Forrest, Santa Rosa Junior College; Virginia Heringer, Pasedena City College; Madeline Fuchs Holzer, New York University; Richard Hood, Denison University; Francis Hubbard, Marquette University; Norma Jaques, Indiana University, South Bend; Richard Larson, Lehman College; Elenore Long, Carnegie–Mellon University; Sarah Hope Parameter, University of California, Santa Cruz; Madeleine Picciotto, Spelman College; Alan Powers, Bristol Community College; Don Rothman, University of California–Santa Cruz; David R. Russell, Iowa State University; Jeff Sommers, Miami University Middletown; Victor J. Vitanza, University of Texas–Arlington; Jacqueline Wilson, Western Illinois University; and Kenney Withers, Southern Illinois University.

Ann Watters
Marjorie Ford

Introduction: Resources for Implementing Community Service Writing

One of the fundamental purposes of the first American universities was to prepare individuals to become good citizens. Recent increases in crime, violence, homelessness, the breakdown of traditional family support systems, and the decline in the quality of our public schools have led many educators and politicians to acknowledge that we are at a crucial juncture in our national history. Now is the time to return to that principle of higher education which emphasizes the role that high schools and universities can play in preparing students to be citizens through service to their communities.

Many of our national and community leaders are implementing new legislation to support such change. For example, the National Community Service Trust Act of 1993 mandates that the states help develop programs that link academic and service learning in order to help solve social problems while preparing students to become better citizens. From Clinton's National Service programs that allow students to defer some of the cost of their college tuition for working in inner cities or communities at risk, to the Summer of Service and Summer of Safety programs, to community service projects that are sponsored by high schools and colleges, this practical and idealistic approach to education will continue to gain advocates.

Service learning encourages students to rethink how they learn and why they value their education. As students become involved in their communities, they become active rather than passive learners. While helping to identify and solve problems in their communities, they are building closer connections between their campus and their communities. Service learning experiences provide unique opportunities to learn about our increasingly varied and changing world, to understand people and cultures that are unique, and to develop resourcefulness, a stronger inner self, a clearer sense of personal identity. More than any other type of educational activity, working with others from a different culture and or economic class can help you to begin to think critically about what you have, what you value, what other individuals in your community have a right to expect, and how you can contribute to your community.

A young teacher whose interview is included in Robert Coles's *The Call of Service* captured one of her first realizations about how tutoring poor children helped her to understand and think about children who are "culturally deprived" in a new light:

I'd never seen where these kids live, how they live. I'd driven by but it's another thing to go and walk up those stairs and be in the apartments. I don't want to be overly dramatic: it's not that I had any trouble, or that what I saw was so surprising or shocking. It's just that I finally began to see, right before my eyes, what separated those kids from me. At first, when I started teaching, I thought that if I could just go back a little to my own childhood and draw on it, then I'd make the connections I needed to make, and things would go well. But once I'd started going to the homes, it sunk in that these kids had to cross lots of bridges to get to me and my childhood, never mind me now. You can read a lot in books about the "culturally deprived child," but when you're sitting on a couch in a ghetto apartment building, looking and listening and wondering and worrying, then it's another story.

As a result of her experience this young woman went on to become one of the leaders in her college's community service project.

We have developed *A Guide from Change* to help you meet the challenges of service learning. This guide focuses on the intellectual concepts, the approaches to critical thinking and reflection, and the practical information that you will need to get started on your journey as a writer who can make an impact on your community. On this journey you will encounter many opportunities to work with others and to write for different groups and types of individuals. At the same time the experiential nature of your projects will often demand that you think clearly and creatively in unanticipated situations. You may have to work in situations and solve problems that you have not yet encountered in your own family, high school, community, or culture. Although facing new situations and working with people who may come from different backgrounds and cultures may be challenging, through these experiences you will become better informed about the ways in which relationships form and develop between individuals and groups—be they social, professional, political, or collegial. As you begin building productive relationships, you will be creating new definitions of community.

As you work in a community organization, you will find yourself rethinking some of the ways in which you think about writing. You will discover that writing effectively for a particular organization in your community requires more than just knowing the principles of logic, style, grammar, and punctuation. You may need to learn how to write in forms other than the essay that you have studied in your writing courses to date. These new forms might well include letters to the editor, interviews, articles for newsletters or journals, informational brochures, fact sheets, or grant proposals. While different from academic writing, these types of writing will help you to realize that whatever you write needs to follow a form that is appropriate to the situation, and that takes the audience's expectations into account. The range of "real writing" that you do for your community organizations and their readers will challenge you to engage the attention of your audience, to inform them honestly, to convince them to listen to your point of view.

In fact, many of our students have been motivated to change their attitudes about the importance of writing because they were writing for a "real" audience. One student shared the important effect that his community service writing project had on his awareness of himself as a person and as a writer:

My community service writing project was a firsthand experience with minority students who were breaking the traditional route of not continuing on to complete a college education. My job was more than observing from afar or talking to the students in light conversation; this was up front and personal. The writing was not difficult, and that may be in large part due to the fact that I had in mind the practical importance of the writing. I knew that this was going to be published and read, and I took it to heart.

What you learn writing for community audiences will help you with the writing that you do for your college courses. While working with and writing for community or campus publications, you will be developing your writing and thinking skills as well as your flexibility and self-confidence.

A Guide for Change has four chapters. Chapter 1 introduces you to the definitions and concepts that support service learning while emphasizing the significant role that reflection has in this learning process. Chapter 2 integrates the practical worksheets with the writing and learning processes that you will find useful as you plan, draft, revise, and evaluate your service learning experiences and projects. Chapter 3 has two casebooks; each takes you step-by-step through students' processes and completion of community service writing projects. Chapter 4 features a variety of models of community service writing projects that were completed by students at the University of Northern Iowa, the University of Miami, and Stanford University.

It is not possible to know where your service learning experiences will lead you. We do know that your journey will be challenging, and we hope that the advice this guide provides will be helpful to you along the way.

Ann Watters
Marjorie Ford

CHAPTER 1

Concepts of Service Learning

Concepts of Service Learning and the Language of Service

We begin this guide with some philosophical and practical observations. The following readings convey different approaches to service learning but evoke common beliefs and values—about the nature of learning; about commitment to personal, educational, and civic values; about the communities in which we live, work, and study.

At the heart of service learning and community service writing is the belief that there are different ways to become engaged in communities, and that when students become genuinely engaged in their communities, not only are they giving, but they are learning as well. Our first selection, an excerpt from *The Call of Service* by physician and educator Robert Coles, captures several students' experiences in community service learning. As you read the Coles selection, reflect on the efforts of people who want to "engage themselves in a broken world and find a place for their moral energy," and consider the ways in which you might be interested in becoming engaged in your local community.

In the next selection, "Service or Censorship? A Relationship Approach to Community Service," Jeremy Cohen, a professor of communication, focuses on the crucial relationship between the community, the students, and the project itself. Drawing from his experience in a communication course with a service component, Cohen discusses engaging his students in critical thinking, reflection, and problem solving as they confront conflicts between "their expectations and their images of what they should be doing" and "the community's perceptions of what needs to be done." Most of all, Cohen illustrates the importance of bringing all participants in community service projects into the discussion to work on issues in a manner that does not create winners and losers, but rather benefits all participants.

Professor Patricia O'Connor's article, "'You Have to Keep Coming Back': The Responsibility of Those Who Serve," discusses both theory and practice in her institution's prison education program. O'Connor captures not only the practical matters—how one dresses, personal safety—but also what her program means to the inmates whom the reading and writing program serves. As one inmate observes, "You've got to come back. There are no new conversations here." O'Connor quotes Ira Harkavy, a leader in community service learning at the University of Pennsylvania, in discussing such college-based programs and the obligations of colleges. "It is the social and necessary imperative of universities to serve communities."

While the three selections discuss both philosophy and experience, the following two sections in Chapter 1, "Questions and Answers about Community Service Writing" and "Research and Service," focus primarily on implementing service learning, particularly in writing courses. "Questions and Answers" discusses not only the types of community service writing but also the ways in which students at a range of institutions, in different types of communities, and with different levels of expertise in writing can develop and engage in projects that teach them while they contribute to the local community or the common good. The section on "Research and Service" discusses ways in which the commonly assigned research paper can both engage students and serve the public interest.

This chapter is designed to open up conversations about community engagement and real-world writing assignments. We hope that, as Professor

O'Connor puts it, many new conversations will ensue—about learning, about writing, and about the ways in which service and learning reinforce each other to the advantage of both students and communities.

CONCEPT AND PRACTICE: THE LANGUAGE OF SERVICE

In order to begin conversations about service and learning, we need to develop a common language. The concept of service and learning goes by many names: service learning, experiential learning, study-service connections, public service, community service, social action, citizen involvement, civic education, field studies, and more. We want to explore a few of the terms most often used in service learning experiences and explain why we have selected those we use.

First, we need to look at the core terms of "community," "public," "service," and "learning." Traditionally, "community" evoked a sense of a geographical region, yet we often speak of "the black community" or "the gay community," even when we are speaking of people from diverse geographical regions; thus, "community," for many, has come to signify shared values and experience. "Public" often means the general public, regardless of shared values, or it can evoke the notion of government service. "Service" is an even more controversial concept, because if there is a server, there is a "servee"; if there is a giver, there is a receiver; if there is a helper, there is a "helpee"—in other words, some inequity exists in the relationship. In the past, "service" has had connotations of menial work; today, "serving the community" has been too often a process whereby well-meaning and well-off individuals seek to go out and "do good." Some educators and community members suggest that when community members themselves haven't been consulted about their needs, the server is in fact serving his or her own needs and wishes. Others point out that the whole notion of service reinforces historical stereotypes about colonialism and ethnic and gender hierarchy.

And finally, the term "learning," a term that should be at the core of any educational enterprise, refers to "the action of receiving instruction or acquiring knowledge . . . a process which leads to the modification of behavior or the acquisition of new abilities or responses and which is additional to natural development by growth or maturation" (*Oxford English Dictionary*). Learning is the aspect of community or public service that balances the "server-servee" equation. In a program of service learning or study-service, students are serving the community, whether directly through service work or less directly through writing for nonprofit community organizations and projects. At the same time they are also learning from the community; the community, in a sense, works with the college in educating society's young people. It is this sense of mutuality, of shared responsibility, of give and take, that supports the ideal service-learning connection.

The terms we focus on in this text are "community service," "service learning," and "study-service connections." When the Community Service Writing Project evolved at our institution, we chose the name to reflect our desire to enable students to write in different discourse communities, both on and off campus, and to reinforce the connections between the academy and its surrounding community. Our use of the terms "service learning" and "study-service connection" reflects, as well, the appropriate goal of college courses with service components: to create opportunities for combining community or public work and academic work in ways that enhance each, while stressing the mutuality of the giving and receiving in any community-based action, whether research, writing, or direct service. If we accept the view of Marian Wright Edelman, in her often quoted line, "Service is the rent we pay for living," we can see service as something we give back for what we have received or are receiving. And if we take the opportunity in journals, discussion sections, essays, and other assignments to examine and reflect on the service experience, we have genuinely engaged in critical thinking, in reading and writing, and in learning.

"Community Service" from *The Call of Service*

Robert Coles

. . . Today's students are likely to express their lofty political and social impulses and practical desires to change the world through community service, even if in limited or modest ways. I have spent many years—since 1978—working with college students engaged in community service; they tutor the young, keep company with the elderly, visit the sick, run summer camps, design and implement educational programs in prisons, help the medically needy and indigent get hospital care, and argue in the courts on behalf of tenants or workers. Often those students experience the same conflicts or misgivings that deeply troubled the activists of the civil rights era and that now trouble older people working full-time as community organizers.

"I want to help the kids I know," a college junior told me, but he had his eye on what he called "the larger picture." When I asked him to fill me in on the details of that picture, he was both voluble and impassioned. "This entire ghetto is a breeding ground of crime, and someday it has to go! Don't ask me how we'll do it, but until the nation addresses the problems here in this ghetto neighborhood, we'll keep having the troubles, the riots, the problems with drugs and violence. I tutor the kids, and I try to tell them there's a better life for them to lead if they'll only study and do well in school. But they only half-believe me when they're young, and when they become teenagers, they're cynical—boy, are they cynical. I guess I'd be if I was living where they are. It's hard for someone like me to argue against that cynicism, so I try to undermine it. I try to be as thoughtful and helpful as I can. I try to keep teaching, and I try to show these kids that there's another world out there, and it's not a totally bad one or a totally callous one. I take them to Cambridge, and I show them that world, and I hope it rubs off on them."

His words spoke of an earnest dedication to children, even those whose prospects seemed poor. This dedication was enabled not by a fatuous refusal to look at a grim social reality, or by a romanticism that proposed salvation through tutoring and friendship. That young man had taken a close, hard look at the obstacles and had told himself (as his work showed) that one person could give direction to another in a classroom, on a playground.

On the other hand, doubts and misgivings asserted themselves again and again. "Sometimes I think I'm just kidding myself. I think I should forget tutoring and mentoring, and field trips and summer camps, and just go to work as a political organizer, something like that—try to change the whole system. If I was a lawyer—I say that a lot out loud to myself: 'If you were a lawyer . . .' But I never really finish the sentence, because I've see the law students come here and take on cases, and what they do seems exciting for a while: fighting against lead poisoning, or dangerous stairways, or rats all over the place, or not enough heat in the winter. But you know, it's like a drop in the bucket: this is a neighborhood of thousands of people, and they're locked in—they just don't seem to be able to break out, and the world I belong to, the white world of affluence and power, that world doesn't really want these folks. Maybe it has no use for them, no jobs for them, though there's prejudice, too, plenty of it.

"My dad says, If a black boy really works hard he can make it, he can go to a good school. He's a trustee of one [a fine New England private school], and he says the school goes begging for black kids, but they're hard to come by. I don't think Dad realizes what those kids have been through by the time they're thirteen or fourteen and old enough to go to high school. A lot of them, they've just surrendered. I've taught them; they're smart, plenty of them are, but they're not 'into' school: it's not their idea of something that will lead to anything. That's what they tell me, and then I talk myself blue in the face, but in the middle I can see they're tuning out on me. That's when I tune out on myself and think of politics or the law—but I'll never go into either."

Nevertheless, he persisted. Twice a week he went to a ghetto school, in spite of an extremely busy academic schedule, to teach math to some fifth graders; sometimes he would bring several of them back to his college dorm for a meal. The commitment was exhilarating as well as exhausting; he took pride in a child's thank-you, a child's declaration that she was doing better in school, a child's wide-eyed awe at the sight of a well-known university, followed by questions about how one gets there and where one goes as a graduate.

Soon we will take a sustained look at the emotional ups and downs of those rendering service, but here I want to describe the efforts of one young woman in college who hadn't considered what community service might be until her boyfriend, a seemingly single-minded premed student, mentioned that he was going to be a Big Brother and do some tutoring.

She said, "We were having coffee at the beginning of school, and he told me he was going to be doing community service. I thought it had something to do with politics, maybe, or some charity, like the Community Fund. I remember looking at him in a different way. I'd never seen that side of him.

"Anyway, the more he told me about community service, the more I wanted to do it. So I volunteered—and here I am. I go to the school one afternoon a week. I sit with kids who are having trouble with their schoolwork. I teach reading and spelling. I try to connect with them—that's the first thing you have to do. If you don't then you might as well go back home and call it quits. I tell them what's happened to me during the week, and I bring goodies, and I've promised the kids that one of these days I'll teach them how to make these oatmeal raisin cookies I make. I bring in some books I used to read when I was their age—well, younger. I can remember Mom or Dad reading the stories to me. It's so sad, though—these kids have never owned a book, never seen a book in their house, never had anyone read to them. They ask me why my parents read to me. I tell them [it was] because they liked to—and they believed reading is important, and it will make a big difference in your life. They aren't convinced, some of them. Others *seem* convinced, but I'm not convinced that they're really convinced. A few—they break my heart—they're really eager, and they're aching, that's the word, *aching* to get out of the ghetto and live someplace else. This girl said to me she wanted to find someplace that's safe, when you can wake up and think you're really going to go to bed that night in your house, and not in the hospital or in a funeral parlor!"

"I really work at the spelling. The kids will ask why—what's such a big deal about spelling the word 'commit' with two *m*'s and one *t*? Why not one *m* and two *t*'s? Why not two *m*'s and two *t*'s? Stop being so uptight, they say to me. I sure don't want to be someone who corrects someone else's spelling, a kid said. How did I answer him? I wasn't sure what to say! I tried the 'rules' strategy: we have to go by the rules, so everyone speaks the same way and reads the same words and spells them the same way.

"The kids really pushed me. They said, So long as you can understand what someone writes—understand the words, then that's all that counts! I gave them a speech about order and predictability, but I remembered my uncle saying that George Bernard Shaw wanted to change the spelling of a lot of words, because spelling is so arbitrary and irrational, and I remembered that Flannery O'Connor hated spelling and deliberately didn't spell a lot of words right. I wouldn't want *her* there when I was teaching the word 'commit' or 'commitment'! She'd probably have spoken up, said 'Hey, I don't have to take this, the way you're spelling that word; I can spell it any which way I want!'"

Yet the young teacher knew that her students needed to learn how to read and write and count and spell; they needed the same educational competence she herself had long ago acquired. She kept working against her students' indifference and surly distrust—and her own sophisticated qualms, her temptation to join those boys and girls, to stoop rebelliously to their cynicism. She kept reminding them and herself that jobs would eventually be at stake, and a distinctly improved standard of living.

"That's what community service is for me, if you want to know: the nitty-gritty of it is getting right in there with the kids, and not only teaching them how to spell 'commit,' and what it means, and 'commitment,' and how to use the word, but getting down in the pit with the kids, and trying to show them you're not some snotty white creep who's loaded with money and wants to make them feel dumb, and then get them to improve, so *she* can feel even smarter than she did before, and be even snottier!

"I'm being vague, I know. What I mean is, you've got to stand up for what you believe in. You've got to tell those kids, Look, this is the English language, and this is how you spell 'commit,' and if you want to be part of our society, our country, then when you see a red light, you stop your car, and when you see someone who is smiling and saying hello, you say hello back, and when you pick up a book, you read it in such a way that you stop if there's a period, and when you write, you begin a sentence with a capital letter, and you spell the word 'sentence' and not 'sentance,' the way my kids there told me they'd like to spell it, and 'commit,' not 'committ.'

"I think they get the message. They may not agree with me, but they realize that I'm putting myself on the line, and trying to reach them and give them some connection to the world of literacy. I really scored when I told the kids that if they knew how to spell 'commit' right, they'd do well in a job if they had to type for someone—and if the person writing misspelled the word, they could say, Hey, that's not spelled right! They got a big kick out of that— the boss-man falling flat on his face. They're used to hearing their parents talk about the know-it-all whites, and know you can't cross them, no matter what. I think they really took to the idea of learning how to spell so you can trip up some honky!"

She was doing her best to enjoy her community service work while at the same time taking it very seriously. That work eventually led to the end of her friendship with her premed classmate. Once, talking about the teaching they did in ghetto schools, he mentioned that this would help him get into medical school. She was appalled—and he was enraged by her dismay and disapproval, her naiveté. Their falling-out affected her work.

"I had more time for the kids. I stopped and asked myself: what do you want to do—jump fast into another relationship or stop for a while and try to figure out what kind of a relationship you want, and meanwhile spend a lot of time with these kids? That way you're becoming *yourself*, not just defining yourself as a college student, or a field hockey player, or someone's girlfriend.

"It was then [after the breakup] that I figured out a way to teach reading better, and spelling. I took a course, and I put more energy and imagination into the class, and there was a big change in the kids: they could see that I was there with them, heart and soul, and they quieted down. When they started making noise, I spoke right up; my voice got tense, and I leveled with them and told them I wasn't there so we could waste time—I had too much respect for them. I really don't think it was *what* I said; I think it was my attitude—my *commitment* (with one *t*!). I told them I thought of them a lot when I read something or saw something on television or heard something over there, back in college, and so they began to pay more and more attention. And then I started making home visits, and did *that* make a big, big difference!"

At first, it made much more difference to her than to the children she was teaching. Her visits to homes were a measure of a new resolution, a step into territory she had only imagined or heard described by the children themselves or by sociologists. Now she was seeing their world firsthand, and now that world lived in her, even when she left it.

"I'd never seen where these kids live, how they live. I'd driven by, but it's another thing to go and walk up those stairs and be in the apartments. I don't want to be overly dramatic; it's not that I had any trouble, or that what I saw was so surprising or shocking. It's just that I finally began to see, right before my eyes, what separated those kids from me. At first, when I started teaching, I thought that if I could just go back a little to my own childhood and draw on it, then I'd make the connections I needed to make, and things would go well. But once I'd started going to the homes, it sunk in that these kids had to cross lots of bridges to get to me and my childhood, never mind me now. You can read a lot in books about 'the culturally deprived child,' but when you're sitting on a couch in a ghetto apartment building, looking and listening and wondering and worrying, then it's another story."

By her senior year she was a leader in her college community service program. She helped other volunteers settle in, helped them as they stumbled and sometimes thought of quitting. She was not interested in the political struggles of the ghetto where she worked, nor did she ever become an "activist," as some of her friends did.

"I'm a teacher here, and it's enough for me to do the best job I can. I have a friend who now wants to go to law school and fight with the school people and fight with the welfare department and fight with the store people and the real estate people. I guess I'm not a fighter. I wish I were sometimes. I'd like to go into court and sue somebody—anybody—for the sake of those kids I teach. But there's room for everybody, I guess. That's what one of the mothers told me when I said I wish I could go and change the world. She said, 'That's all right, you *are* changing the world!' Hearing her say that was like getting all A's on a report card."

I began to realize that she was telling me of more than a shift in activity. To be sure, she had learned how to become more effective, more knowledgeable about the children she intended to inform and even inspire. Yet she herself was being informed and inspired. It was an awakening of sorts, a change of moral direction.

The phrase "community service" these days commonly refers to the work done by young volunteers: high school and college students working in schools, hospitals, soup kitchens, nursing homes, or prisons. They help at camps and on playgrounds, visit homes and neighborhoods with books and instruction manuals, with basketballs and footballs and baseballs. Older people render community service in those same places and in other ways, too. When I talked with men and women at a General Motors factory in Framingham, Massachusetts, I got to know blue-collar and white-collar workers who proudly mentioned their community service. They described work with Boy Scouts, Girl Scouts, Little Leaguers; they talked about their visits to hospitals and nursing homes; they mentioned cleanup drives, weekend efforts to make streets, parks, and playgrounds clean and attractive.

A thirty-year-old assembly-line worker spoke with great feeling of his weekly visit to a nursing home two miles from his home. "I got into it by a fluke; a buddy of mine had to put his dad away in one of them, and he got all upset. He didn't have much money, and the place wasn't good. The only good thing about it, some people came and read to the old folks, and brought them cookies and cake, and just sat with them and watched TV with them and talked with them. They'd play checkers or cards, nothing fancy, and show them pictures of their family—shoot the breeze. Then my buddy's dad just suddenly died one day, and that was it. But for my friend it was hard to get that nursing home out of his mind. He talked with the priest; he told him he'd wake up in the middle of the night, and he'd be thinking of his dad—that's normal, that's grieving for you—but he'd be thinking of that nursing home, all those folks. It was sad. So the priest said, Maybe the thing to do is go and visit one of those homes, and see if you can be of help, and that way you'll feel you're doing something good, something worthwhile—and it could be a kind of memorial to the old man. And my friend, he really liked that idea.

"So that was how it got started. He talked to me, and I said yes, and he and I went to this nursing home, and we told them we aren't anyone special, but we like to have fun, and we could try to give the folks in there a good time. We could bring them some cookies, and we can sing—I can sing a lot of songs, and my friend plays the piano (no big deal, but the tune gets across!) and we could always read from the papers, if someone was blind or had the shakes and couldn't hold the paper steady. They were glad we came—they said visitors really help the people, and the staff, too. So we started, and we weren't sure at first what we were going to do, and we were nervous, to start, but we just decided we'd be ourselves and try to be as friendly as we knew how, and my wife made these cookies, and I just went and offered them around, and they all told us to come back, and we did, and now we're regulars and we love it—it's part of our lives. You give something, and believe me, you get something back."

He was too modest to mention that he had urged others to work with the elderly or with young people in trouble with the law, with drugs and drinking. In fact, he always pointed to the initiatives, activities, and good ideas of friends of his, working men who made it their business to give time and energy to others. When a local paper wanted to highlight his volunteer efforts, he insisted that he be mentioned only as part of a group. And he urged that their work *not* be called community service.

"It's more a person-to-person thing, and it's us trying to be friendly to people who aren't having the best of times. I know, it does help everyone—the community—when you go and visit the old folks, but I don't think of it as service. To me, service means, like, the military, or you're doing something you've *got* to do, or you've been *told* to do it, or you've been *sentenced* to it, because you got in trouble with the law. To me, what we do is—well, it's us trying to offer something from our hearts, only we all got together, and we're organized about it."

He could have been speaking for many of the college students and older people who have the impulse to engage themselves in a broken world and find a place for their moral energy.

Service or Censorship?
A Relationship Approach to Community Service

Jeremy Cohen

The *Informer,* a single-sheet, two-sided newspaper produced by seventh and eighth graders, sits in the corner of an office at the intermediate school. It will not be circulated until the offending story has been blacked out.

My university journalism students, who are volunteering their time to supervise the paper and teach the younger students, see this as censorship. Perhaps even a violation of the First Amendment. *Congress shall make no law . . . abridging the freedom of speech, or of the press.* They worry that their community service project is in jeopardy. Their expectations are bruised.

"Mrs. T," the intermediate school teacher who asked my students for help, sees her decision to delete the article as living up to her responsibilities as a classroom teacher. "I hope you understand the ramifications of our actions here," she says to my community service volunteers.

The article? It was written by Ben, a thirteen-year-old, and says the school's new computers, donated by a corporate sponsor, "mean we can play more games and it goes faster so we don't have to wait long." Mrs. T does not want sponsors to think their gifts are used for games. Among her concerns are the messages sent to audiences beyond the schoolhouse gate.

Welcome to the world of community service. It plays havoc with expectations. It is messy. It lays bare the consequences of what seems dry and theoretical in the classroom. When you make the most of it, it works. But it works to what? Who is being *served?* What *is* community service?

Community service is a relationship. It includes you and some members of a community. It is important to think of it as a relationship because your actions are going to do something—help or hinder, benefit or waste time that belongs to you and to others. Explicit in this relationship is the attempt to engage in activities that the community believes are useful. Heroes charging in on white chargers are not useful. In the community service relationship, there is a partnership in which you can bring your own talents to bear working with the community only at the invitation of the community. Developing a productive relationship, then, first requires listening to the community—riding in slowly and working with others to identify the kinds of things that really need to be done.

There is a second and very important dimension to the community service relationship when students are involved. It goes by the shorthand "service education." This relationship consists of your efforts as a student to work with the community in a way that recognizes explicit academic and curricular roots planted deeply in your own home school. Community service is a *good* thing. The school's responsibility, however, is to do more than *good*. It is to create an environment with the highest likelihood for learning. And as it so happens, service education–based community service does just that.

My journalism students, for example, are using their own classroom knowledge of news gathering, writing, editing, ethics, and press law as they work with the community. If the relationship works, the community will benefit and my students will have a much stronger grasp themselves of the social forces James Madison confronted when he crafted the First Amendment in 1789. Freedom of expression in Mrs. T's class is no longer an ideal in a text. It is a real-life issue and, at least for the seventh- and eighth-grade *Informer* reporters, the way my journalism students act on that ideal will have consequences.

My journalism students call an eight o'clock evening meeting to consider the issues and the options. They are angry. They are agitated. They view Mrs. T as an unreasonable censor.

"How are we supposed to teach our students journalism if she is going to censor them?" they demand. Their question *seems* reasonable. In the classroom, I might suggest an answer. They are, after all, supposed to learn from my lectures. The schools may not censor except to preserve academic order or prevent physical or psychological harm, I would say in my press law class. Or, I could encourage my students to consider the canons of freedom of expression. Discern the answers from the past, I might tease while directing them toward John Milton's "Areopagitica." "*And though all the winds of doctrine were let loose to play upon the earth, so Truth be in the field, we do injuriously by licensing and prohibiting to misdoubt her strength,*" Milton wrote. "Is Mrs. T so afraid of Ben's *truth*—that for children, computers represent play as well as work?" asks Michael, the journalism student who helped to organize our community service initiative.

Unfortunately, these are the wrong questions. "How are we supposed to teach journalism if . . ." carries an underlying assumption by my students that they are riding into Mrs. T's classroom on white chargers. The quest they are voicing is their quite honorable desire to teach the *Informer* reporters what they are themselves learning in their university journalism classes. Michael and the others want to defend the besieged students from the horns of the censor. "Is Mrs. T so afraid . . ." relates well to Milton and to Madison's vision of the First Amendment as an open marketplace of ideas, yet the question's relation to community service is questionable.

The problem is that my students' expectations and their images of what they should be doing have come face-to-face with the community's perception of what needs to be done. They are not the same. My students want to teach journalism as a search for truth. Mrs. T wants the *Informer* students to have a positive experience producing a newspaper. My students want to defend Ben's right to talk about the way he uses computers. Mrs. T wants to teach the *Informer* students that technology represents more than play, and she would like the *Informer* to send that message to the corporate sponsor as well. My students see this as an issue of censorship. Mrs. T sees this as . . . Stop!

The question for community service volunteers is not, how do *you* see the issue? It is, how does the community view the issues at hand? Why did the community ask for your help? What is the common thread between your desire to help the community and the community's invitation to you?

Underneath all of the apparent differences between Mrs. T and my students is the most basic issue—something that we can in fact treat as the common thread that generates both a willingness to serve and an invitation from the community to lend a hand. The common ground for Mrs. T and my students is Ben and the other *Informer* reporters. More important than classroom sponsors, truth, and censorship? Stop!

The relationship among truth, censorship, corporate sponsors, and computer games is not a hierarchical one—at least not within the context of community service. It is not useful to think of these issues as representing ends of a spectrum or even as carrying ethical values in one direction or another. That is not to say that censorship is unimportant or that I want my journalism students to act as censors. It is just that these are issues that cannot be tackled from atop a white horse.

Community service has a long tradition of success based on the creation of individual relationships and the use of those relationships to work on issues of mutual concern. For my journalism students, seeing the creation and nurturing of relationships with Mrs. T and with the seventh and eighth graders is the goal. Among community organizers this is known as *"bringing everyone to the table,"* and the reason behind this tactic is simple. As long as everyone is at the table—Mrs. T, the *Informer* staff, the university community service students—there is a chance to tackle the important issues in a manner in which everyone benefits. Ordering issues such as censorship and truth so that whatever decisions are made creates winners and losers—Mrs. T or the community service students—guarantees an end to friendly relations and an end to the possibility of long-term benefit. But so long as we are all at the table, there is time to work on long-term goals.

The relationship approach of community service also recognizes that the goal is not to have a few volunteers slay a community's dragon. In this case, the goal is not to get Ben's story about the computers published. Rather, the goal is to work with Mrs. T and with the students in a way that will give them the tools they will need to succeed without the volunteers.

The agitation and the anger the volunteers feel fades as they think about the ways they can use their relationships with Mrs. T and the students in a positive way. The issue turns from censorship to teaching.

"What about pasting a label over the offending article?" Michael says. "And on the label we could have a simple thank-you to the company that donated the computers. Then there would be no objection to distributing the *Informer*."

"Isn't that still censorship?" another student asks.

"Not if we have the *Informer* students make it clear that the article is an advertisement or an editorial rather than news," Michael says. "And this way we can begin a lesson on the difference between opinion and news that meets our teaching goals and allows Mrs. T to clear the censorship hurdle."

The group is working now. The talk turns to brainstorming about future issues of the *Informer*. The threat of censorship disappears because what caused it was not Mrs. T's desire to sanitize Ben's article, but rather an earlier over-sight—the volunteers' failure to talk with Mrs. T and her students about the differences between news and opinion.

The volunteers were ready to go to the wall when they thought they were being asked to support a censor. As well they should. They were able to dis-mantle the wall, however, when they put aside confrontation for the relation-ship approach of community service.

The *Informer* will find its way into the marketplace of ideas in a couple of days. The community service volunteers will chalk up a victory over the cen-sor's blade and view Milton, Madison, and the First Amendment a little diff-erently than they did before. And the new and stronger relationship among Mrs. T, the *Informer* reporters, and the community service volunteers will be there as a foundation for the next crisis. And that is a good thing because a reliable source tells me that Ben has a story in mind about the corrupt wheel-ings and dealings of the seventh-grade student council.

"You Have to Keep Coming Back": The Responsibility of Those Who Serve

Patricia E. O'Connor

I got involved in prison work because for several years my employer, George-town University, had been developing a relationship with Lorton Prison through law student counseling and course work on "street law." In 1983 a group of philosophy students expanded on that service involvement and began a reading and discussion course with inmates in the all-male Maximum Secur-ity Unit. In 1985 the inmates, pleased with this reading group, requested the chance to try college-level courses. They had all passed their tests for General Education Development (GED) for a high school equivalency, and the prison's higher education program did not service their branch of the complex housing the District of Columbia's (then) 9000 prisoners. Thus, a volunteer service was the springboard for an educational service. The philosophy students asked me, then a coordinator of G.U.'s Writing Program and formerly a teacher of inner-city youth, to teach the first college credit–bearing course in "Max."

I think it is important that the inmates made the request for college course-work, that they asked for more structure and more difficult work, perhaps in spite of an assumption that they might not be ready for a Georgetown class. With an anonymous donation and the backing of the G.U. School for Summer and Continuing Education, we began with one course, "Composition and

Literature," and with time grew to include courses in poetry/drama, short story/novel, philosophy and ethics, philosophy of science, American history, and accounting.

I used that first writing course to test the waters. I discovered students with a wide range of abilities and a serious lack of confidence. Yet these men were an extraordinary group of close readers—close readers who were frank about what they did not understand and quick to relate what they did to the world inside the prison walls. For example, one night inmate James Coward told me he had to turn his back in the noisy Cellblock 5 TV room to cry as he read Antoine de St. Exupery's Little Prince's words to the fox: "It is lonely in the desert: It is lonely in the world of men." The class around him could have been a Greek chorus as they joined in that refrain: "It *is* lonely in the world of men." This message in fact might more appropriately fit the sign we walk under each week as we enter the prison through the iron-clanging gate in the thirteen-feet-deep, thirty-feet-high walls, a sign that says "*Welcome* to Maximum Security."

Today my understanding of prison education and service are enriched by those voices, voices of inmates who developed a sense of their own stories alongside the autobiographical, philosophical, and fictional texts of "established" authors and alongside the very different lives of the Georgetown student volunteers who tutored in these classes. What had happened? We had begun to read deeply, to think deeply, and to write deeply. The assignment that began so simply with a request to "tell a story about your life or someone you know that others can learn from" may have been the catalyst. Or perhaps it was the challenge when I said, "Who, if not you, will write the literature of your experience?" But the actual stories became invitations into the sharing of autobiographical experiences, and perhaps into the joint construction of memory itself. It is part of the joy and the sorrow of service that we are constantly at such difficult intersections in the differing lives of our communities.

But how do we conduct ourselves at the intersections of disparate lives? Our prison service courses are constructed in such a way that Georgetown students participated as volunteers assisting in small-group discussions and participating in one-on-one interaction with inmates about the writing and the understanding of the tasks and texts. Those discussions, as well as the interactive approach to negotiating jointly the meanings of the writings, brought a new kind of talk to the cell block.

WAYS OF CONDUCTING YOURSELF
IN SERVICE TO OTHERS

What I tell volunteers unfamiliar with a prison is to become keen observers and keen listeners. In training and orientation I tell them we must realize that our whole persons are texts being "read" by others. We must listen to people's ways of speaking and make the extra effort to understand words spoken softly, perhaps without eye contact, or in patterns and styles that are new to the listener. I note that this "hard listening" is going on on both sides of the conversations. To help us become better listeners, we speak one-on-one and often. I ask the volunteers to write down names on informal seating charts to remember them. For people who are officially known by numbers, the remembering of a name is a great courtesy.

Part of orientation to service also includes learning from those who receive the service, getting help from them on ways to better orient the new volunteers. I always designate men inside the prison to help recruit other student-inmates and to help prepare them for ways of properly conducting themselves in the cramped eight-foot-by-twelve-foot room that becomes our classroom.

I remind the G.U. students to dress neatly. Many of the inmates arrange to shower and try to have their clothes pressed before they come to our class, showing how highly they value and respect our presence. I ask that volunteers dress simply and unprovocatively so that we do not cause difficulties, especially with prisoners not in our class who see us enter. Those who know us little may do only a "surface" reading of us as texts, reducing us to stereotypes as "females," "arrogant college guys," etc., much in the same way that we see those locked up as all the same, rather than as the individuals we can each become with the familiarity of a shared educational goal.

PERSONAL SAFETY

We do our program in a maximum security unit where offenders are serving long sentences, are in protective custody, or are considered violent offenders who may endanger others. Being alert and cautious is a way of life in prisons, where everyone soon learns to watch the hands of others, for it is with hands that lives are endangered. We distribute to our volunteers safety information and articles on local prison violence in an effort to disclose fully the possibility for danger that is inherent in prison service. The biggest protection in this situation is that afforded by the dignity with which we conduct the tutoring and instruction. Programs that continue for long terms, with consistency and constancy, instill trust and command respect. I also warn the tutors not to overreact, not to be "looking for trouble," because the prisoners themselves screen the participants in our programs as much as possible.

I tell the volunteers that prisons are frightening, but prisoners who respect us for "being about education" are no threat. Feeling uncomfortable may reveal simple, first-time tutoring nervousness. On the other hand, I also warn tutors that a sense of discomfort may reveal a real issue. For instance, one student anguished for some time over how closely an inmate sat beside her. We discussed that if personal space is being violated, we should talk candidly about not ignoring affronts by saying respectfully, but directly, "I'm uncomfortable sitting that close." Prisoners also have their own sense of decorum and protocol. They have found the quietness on the part of some of the new tutors a signal of rudeness or fear. To create a climate of comfort, we routinize the opening of class by individually greeting the participants. Inmates and tutors shake hands, all introducing ourselves and chatting. And we talk openly about classroom dynamics, difficult tutoring and learning situations, inappropriate remarks, or queries for addresses or phone numbers. We are constantly reminded of the curious paradox of dealing sincerely and safely with individuals whose new desire to progress academically and whose past criminal acts have created a difficult dynamic. Open discussion, well-planned and full assignment plans, and commitment to the longevity of this now nine-year-old program have done much to quell the few small but troubling one-on-one difficulties.

REFLECTIONS ON SERVICE

We keep a collaborative journal that records impressions of the class and the tutoring, memorable moments and comments, attendance of both tutors and inmates, difficulties and delights of the experience. This journal, kept for several years, helps us select issues for training and discussion. Absence often reveals much about both campus and prison life which affects the planning and implementation of course work and methods. We from the university grow in knowledge of new terminologies: Men are in "A.S." (administrative segregation), "the hole," or "S.A." I discovered on inquiry that S.A. was a rather elaborate pun on the prison's A.S. category. When inmates were sent into confinement or far off to other states or counties where prisons and jails have cell space for rent, some inmates labeled that metaphorically as a move to Saudi Arabia and thus S.A.! When "locked down" for involvement in an incident (arguments over phone use or television stations are common) an inmate cannot attend educational programs. The journal records this temporary change and lets tutors know that work should be sent to that inmate for completion outside class. Inmates learned through the occasional tutor absence of the students' mid-term exam load, research papers due in several classes at once, and the pressures of graduate school applications. Thus, in the journal we record the day-to-day learning. But most of all, in the journal we find the voices of the student volunteers and the inmates, curious and caring, amazed and proud at small moments: "They've obviously debated all week in the cellblock about that line in the play!" or in sympathy, "XXX was denied parole this week. He's really feeling low, had done none of the assignment."

Some students who volunteer for this prison work are also writing papers that connect their involvement with a course they take on campus, perhaps a course in theology, philosophy, psychology, English, or sociology. They write of the connections they see between classroom readings, theories of behavior, or systems of belief, and what they observe of prison life during their volunteer experience. In some cases this can be counted as a fourth credit, similar to a lab in a science course. Indeed, Lee Shulman of Stanford University, addressing participants in the 1991 Campus Compact Institute for Service Learning, argued that service is the "clinical component of the liberal arts." Some students whose majors may be in government or history make connections by doing research into laws, courts, or histories of particular institutions, to better understand the complexities of communities dealing with rising rates of crime and punishment as they symbiotically operate in modern societies. Others, often English majors, make collections (with permission) of prisoners' poems and other writings, typing and binding the inmates' works as culminating projects for the men who have little access to typing and word processing. Collaborating on a brochure or photo essay to describe our prison education program is a current project in writing and reflection. What holds together all this experience of teaching, tutoring, writing, and collaborating on learning is what Robert Coles describes as the "call of service" that we see in the exchange of voices, the sharing of new experiences, the joint construction of knowledge.

NO NEW CONVERSATIONS

One hundred-degree summer day long after our program had shut down for the year and our tutors had left for summer jobs, vacations, or postgraduate study, I received a call from Tony Mo, a man who had told me how he bragged that he was a "Man" for doing time at "Max."

Tony Mo said, "Ms. O, Ms. O, you've got to come back."

I answered, "I guess it's pretty awful there in the summer."

He said, "It's not that, Ms. O. You've got to come back. There are no new conversations here."

"There are no new conversations here." One of many lines, simple, elegant. One of many lines that keep echoing long after they are spoken, an echo that serves as a reminder of what a commitment service is. When I recruit tutors I tell them of activist educator Herman Blake (now at Indiana University–Purdue University, Indianapolis) who, when he worked in South Carolina rural communities, asked his students to make a five-year service commitment. I tell them that service without engagement, without commitment, verges on voyeurism. Quoting Tony Mo, or with him to assist in orientation, I tell them that we are in the business of making new conversations. Recalling the words of West Philadelphia Improvement Corps founder, Ira Harkavy (of the University of Pennsylvania), I tell them that it is the social and necessary imperative of universities to serve communities.

Such a service literacy builds and builds from language learning in our families, on our streets, to school basics, and on into the very fabric of social discourse. Once begun, we must remain committed to promoting engaged service, not only by developing the learner, but by helping the learner to share in the construction of learning and living for others, creating situations for service that continue long after university students graduate and long after prisoners finish "serving" time in prisons. Service to others is a way of looking at and living in the world.

"CARRY IT ON"

"There's a voice within me saying: Carry it on, carry it on," says the Gil Turner lyric that activist folk singer Joan Baez included on her 1969 *One Day at a Time* album. That message during the civil rights days echoes anew in service learning: "When you can't go on any longer, take the hand of your brother. Every victory brings another. Carry it on, carry it on." Service becomes a model to carry to others. Learning to write the stories of one's own experience, learning to analyze and challenge the ideas of Plato's Socrates, learning that Plato's Shadow World is all too real to men who personally know chains, we who tutored or were taught in prison began an exchange that needed to go further. The inmates sought an audience for stories that others could learn from. By their own request, that audience was the youth of the District of Columbia who so obviously are experiencing a speeded-up version of these inmates' paths into crime and into the prison mill.

Thus this service, like that of the Georgetown Law students before, led to the formation of another service. Our inside program wanted to make connections with and serve the community outside the 30-foot walls. I must leave to the future the results of that involvement, sponsored at present by the D.C. Service Corps and Georgetown University School for Summer and Continuing Education. This cooperative involvement joins youth offenders, District of Columbia students, G.U. students, and Maximum Security inmates who will in the coming semesters communicate in person, in letter, and on videotape to connect the prison and the community in studies of prison issues and literature.

In service, community members meet and affect each other. Programs grow and wane as needs and resources grow and wane. In doing service learning, we contribute to the social construction of communities of knowledge. What we are doing then in service is all about change; it is all about making and continuing new conversations.

Sources

Baez, Joan. "Carry It On." Lyrics by Gil Turner. On *One Day at a Time* (album). Vanguard, 1969.

Coles, Robert. *The Call of Service: A Witness to Idealism.* Boston: Houghton Mifflin, 1993.

Benson, Lee, and Ira Harkavy. "Progressing Beyond the Welfare State." *Universities and Community Schools.* Vol. 2, No. 1–2 (1991): 2–28.

Shulman, Lee. "Professing the Liberal Arts." Lecture, Campus Compact Institute on Integrating Service with Academic Study. Stanford, Calif., 1991.

Questions and Answers about Community Service Writing

Students and teachers interested in developing community service writing in their courses will have a number of questions on the theory and practice of this approach. Below are some frequently asked questions and our responses.

1. What is real-world or community service writing?

Community service writing (CSW) is writing for an audience composed of not only your instructor and peers but also others outside your classroom, either the general public or the readers of materials distributed by a community group. CSW is writing that discusses an issue of public interest or concern, or it is writing for or on behalf of a group that serves the public interest.

2. What types of writing projects do students complete for community service writing?

A CSW assignment could be a letter to the editor on a national, local, or campus issue to inform the public or persuade others to take an interest or follow a course of action. A related assignment is an Op-Ed ("opposite the editorial page") essay, similar to a letter to the editor, that tackles a public issue. One student, for example, wrote an Op-Ed piece about legislation regarding hunger and homelessness issues pending in the state legislature; she wrote the Op-Ed piece as an assignment for the Hunger and Homelessness Coalition of a county near her college.

More typically, CSW assignments involve writing on behalf of nonprofit community organizations. Many students write newsletter articles for community agency newsletters, such as the Reach Out newsletter included in this guide, which are distributed to the group's members or to the donors or supporters of such an agency. Often the head of such an agency would have several articles in mind for an upcoming issue and would ask students which of several topics interest them. You might write up an interview with one of the recipients of aid from the organization, or profile one of the organization's leaders or board members. Or you could examine legislation that could affect the organization's constituents and write up an analysis of that legislation for the organization.

Some agencies ask students to do research or to revise and update agency materials. Students sometimes work in the library, as did some students who wrote natural histories about zoo animals; others might make phone calls to gather data, as did two students gathering research on behalf of the Sierra Club on biomass energy. Another student researched drug trafficking between the United States and Mexico and wrote up a documented, analytical essay on the subject for a think tank. Frequently, students can help revise and update an organization's annual report, an activity that teaches them about sources, revision, and clear, concise, and accurate writing.

3. How do I identify or decide upon a topic for my community service writing project?

First of all, you could research an issue that concerns you, then write up an article and submit it to the local or campus newspaper. Choose a subject that will concern others as well as yourself. Do you think orientation for first-year students should be changed? Do you think the college's core requirements need revision? Notice that both issues could concern large numbers of students and both issues are substantive enough to generate some debate. Do you see a lack of interest in political matters on campus or in the neighborhood? Do you see a situation in your community that needs attention, and perhaps research? If so, a letter or essay for the local paper could stimulate some discussion.

In addition to writing about issues for a general, educated audience, you could put your writing skills to work elsewhere on campus or in a community group. Opportunities to write for public audiences vary by region and by community, but nearly every neighborhood or campus will have some need for your work. Are you interested in environmental issues? If so, surely there is a campus or local or regional branch of an environmental organization that would welcome your assistance with writing or researching. Are you concerned about how public schools are doing their job in your community? Are you concerned about crowded classrooms? If so, perhaps you could learn more by tutoring students younger than you in their writing or other course work. You could also keep a log of your experiences and, after spending some time at the school, you might have some ideas about ways to improve some of the problems you have identified; you could share your ideas with the teacher and with school administrators, or perhaps in a public debate about education in your community.

Do you have an assistance agency, a medical auxiliary, or local shelters in your area? Are you in a church or temple community? Are there local schools? Is there a historical society? A county hospital? In addition to offering to help prepare educational or informative materials, you could draft public service announcements for radio, an interesting prospect especially if you're considering a major in journalism. You might also consider a television editorial or "speak out" type program on the local television station on a subject of interest or concern in your community. Does your state, local, or U.S. representative have offices in the vicinity? You could offer to do research or to draft letters to or materials for constituents; regardless of your or the representative's political party, such work gets you writing for diverse audiences and helps keep you informed about public issues. Do you have a city or town council? You could offer to attend meetings and write up summaries to supplement official minutes, especially summaries on specific issues affecting particular groups in the community. See the section on "Action Research" starting on page 29 in this chapter for additional ideas for finding placements.

4. How can I arrange a study-service connection at a nonprofit or community group?

Some schools have a campus office dedicated to field studies or practicum training; others have volunteer offices that can help you connect with a community site. Some students may want to develop their own placements. Your teacher can help you as well. Perhaps she or he will have done some of the initial planning for such placements.

5. How can I be sure that my writing skills are good enough to be published?

First of all, the way to improve writing is to write, and writing for diverse audiences will stretch and stimulate your skills immeasurably. The practice writing done in the classroom is essential, but there is nothing like the motivation of having to write well, having to make yourself clear and comprehensible to someone who won't grade you but will listen with interest to what you are trying to say. Since you will want to be understood, you will do your best to write concisely and clearly, and you will no doubt make fewer mistakes than you might if you felt your writing did not really matter.

But on to the practical matters. Suppose you really do have a spelling problem, or you simply have a hard time combining clauses effectively, or devising clear opening sentences, or choosing the words that would be most appropriate to the audience for your writing. Some students have found it extremely helpful to work collaboratively, to have either a partner or a peer group with whom to exchange materials, help edit, and generally offer mutual support. Many campuses also have peer tutors or drop-in hours for writing tutors. In any case, your instructor will probably want to see any drafts you are ready to submit to an organization or other audience outside your classroom. Be sure to type up a clean draft and go over it with your instructor or other designated person before sharing it with your community "editor," who will also review it and suggest revisions before publication or circulation.

6. How will I fit community service writing in with my other course work?

CSW will often be one of several assignments. It can be more work, but most students feel that the benefits make the project worth the effort. Generally, the assignment will be a substitute for a more traditional essay that your instructor would have required.

What you select or find to do for the assignment really dictates how much time you spend. A report that will become a newsletter article sometimes requires an interview or a few phone calls. On the other hand, the advantage is that you have material with which to write; you aren't searching for an idea to write about, waiting for inspiration until the night-before-the-essay-is-due adrenaline finally gets you worked up enough to write something, anything. While a newsletter article that you submit instead of another essay may require additional time invested early in the process, it can save you some time in the home stretch. It can also help you learn techniques for conducting research, such as interviewing authorities on a subject, that are not always required in a composition class but that are often expected later on in your academic career.

Suppose you have been assigned an argumentative essay for your course. You are to select an issue and argue a point about it. You are to imagine an opposition and argue a point with that opposition. Again, such practice writing has its place, but how much more engaging, how much more interesting, and, in some ways, how much easier to write an argument on an issue you really care about, with real-world consequences, for real readers? That is the situation you have when you write an argument for a public audience on an issue of public concern. Such an assignment could be an Op-Ed piece, but it could also be an argument for peers to stop abusing diet pills or alcohol, or to stop practicing unsafe sex. It could be a grant proposal to a funding source asking for $15,000 so a shelter in your community can keep its doors open next winter. In such assignments, the usual advice about writing arguments matters immensely: anticipate reader objections, watch your tone and word choice, consider your reader's background and point of view.

7. I work, take care of a family, and go to school. How can I possibly find the time to do service learning?

Students lead busy lives, but there are several options for linking field experience or service work to your academic studies. If you can't go out and work with a nonprofit organization and collaborate with other students, you could write a letter to the editor, for your campus or local paper, on an important issue of public concern. For example, do you have feelings about the adequacy of campus day care for students and staff?

Another way to cope with extreme time demands is to do a one-day service project registering voters, participating in a citywide cleanup, planting flowers at the local elementary school, sharing an interest of yours with younger students. You could then write about your experience in your journal or in an essay.

As discussed above, you can use your course assignments that are already required, such as research papers, to investigate issues for a local community group or government agency—utilization of shelters in the area, for example, or successful programs promoting carpooling in other communities, or community programs to combat drug trafficking. Such work helps the assignments you are already doing serve an additional purpose: informing you and others about community issues and providing useful information to local groups.

8. How do I arrange to meet with people off campus? I don't have a car.

If transportation is a problem, consider working with a campus group or one in the immediate vicinity. Often students work in peer groups with organizations off campus, and the chances are that someone in your group will have access to a car. Sometimes campus volunteer bureaus have a van that you can borrow for school-related projects such as your community service writing meetings. Some agency leaders are willing to come to campus to meet student groups, though most are extremely overworked and pressured for time. Those who do agree to host students are excited about the possibility and will make every effort to link up with you to help get your job done. Finally, check to see if you could take public transportation. If you are working in pairs or small groups, you can use the transit time to coordinate your efforts on the project.

Frequently, students only need two or three meetings at the community site: the initial meeting with an agency leader and then one or two follow-up meetings to go over drafts. The final project can often be mailed or faxed in if that is more convenient.

9. I would like to do direct service or volunteer work and write about the experience. What if I encounter cultural or socioeconomic differences or language barriers?

Talk ahead of time with the people who helped to arrange your placement. Develop an understanding of the "ecology" of the community site: the staff, the clients or participants, and any other people who have a stake or interest in your service. Find out who is involved in the proceedings of the organization, why people are there, what their motivations are for being involved in the organization or for utilizing its services. Use your journal to help you reflect on and make sense of these observations. It can help if you accept that there are differences between you and those with whom you are working yet understand that you give to and learn from each other; in other words, each individual can bring something valuable to the interaction, so recognize not only any service you may be rendering but also the insights and experience that you are gaining from those with whom you work.

In terms of cultural differences, be aware that there are different interpersonal styles that may be reflected by the significance of eye contact, body contact, speaking, and learning. Observe the behavior that others at the site model in working with their clients, and when in doubt, ask for guidance. In terms of language, you may be able to recall some of your language training from high school, or maybe you will be motivated to take additional language courses in college. Sometimes nonverbal communication will help; other times, you can use the opportunity to learn or teach another language. Also, see the intercultural worksheet in Chapter 2.

10. What if the agency I work with has a political orientation I don't share?

College and study-service connections are about being exposed to different, new ideas and being challenged to think about social and/or political contexts other than those to which you have already been exposed. Your exposure to different views can provide material for reflection and critical thinking on both your beliefs and those you confront in the community. This doesn't mean that you will be expected to reject your own values. One student who got involved with Salvadoran workers and wrote a newsletter article on a Congressional bill learned a great deal about labor and immigration issues. This young Republican didn't change his political views, but he expanded his knowledge base, listened to opposing views, and grew much better informed about social issues.

11. What if I am asked to produce writing with a political slant?

First of all, discuss the situation with your instructor, your peers, and your agency leader. Such a situation offers a valuable opportunity to reflect critically and carefully on the social context of the nonprofit organization, the audiences for the writing, the agenda of the agency, and your own values. Write frequently and fully in your journal and keep track of your concerns and your reflections. After this necessary first step, you have several options. If you have examined both sides of the argument in question and you still feel that you cannot fulfill your writing assignment, you could ask for a different assignment, explaining why you feel uncomfortable with what you have been asked to do. In some cases you may prefer to write an essay or letter about the situation and address it to your agency leader. One student we know was asked to interview young women at a home for juvenile offenders and write an upbeat article on the great place they lived in. After interviewing the young people at the home, the student writer felt she could not present the situation in the light the agency leader had asked for and expected. After consultation with her instructor, she wrote a letter to the agency explaining why she decided not to write the article in question. The student, the instructor, the young people, and the agency staff all benefited, if a bit painfully, from her insights; the student-writer also learned how to negotiate a very delicate rhetorical situation, to disagree gracefully and respectfully.

12. What if I have to miss a deadline?

In a word, *don't*. People are counting on you and on your writing. You can't simply request an incomplete, or provide a weak excuse. The best way to avoid this situation is to plan ahead: take on only what you can deliver; work with your agency and your instructor to devise a reasonable schedule; and keep in touch with your peer group to make sure everyone is keeping up with his or her part. Allow more time than you think you will need to get in touch with agency people, peers, and your instructor. If an unforeseen situation does develop, get in touch with your agency, peers, and instructor immediately to make alternate plans. Don't avoid the problem. If you are called out of town, at least make one phone call to one of the other people involved in your project to let him or her know your situation. Always remember that you are representing your institution and your program; you are on a job, so you are no longer just a student, and you must be as professional and conscientious as you are able to be.

13. How do I evaluate the relevance of what I am learning?

Potentially, CSW can teach you not only about writing in a variety of forms and for different audiences but also about social issues and community concerns. In addition to the feedback you will get on your written assignments from your instructor, peers, and agency personnel, you may also want to participate in an evaluation process for the whole project. The process could involve journal writing to reflect on what you are learning, or an evaluation sheet you fill out to inform your instructor or agency about the pros and cons of your specific assignment and placement. Or perhaps you could participate in a larger effort by your instructor, the college, and the organization to evaluate what you are learning and what you are contributing to others through your writing. Many instructors assign reflective essays to help you to integrate course readings, other assignments, and your field experiences and to analyze what you have learned both from CSW and from the course as a whole.

In spite of the many challenges you may face as you pursue service learning experiences, you will find many academic and personal rewards that more than compensate for the time and energy such projects can involve. You will find yourself engaged intellectually, academically, and personally in a manner that would be difficult to duplicate in other kinds of courses.

Research and Service

Not only can research skills help you to develop sound essays supported with credible evidence for your college courses, they can also serve the needs of nonacademic communities. As a college student you learn to conduct research and to write up your findings in order to inform yourself and to contribute to knowledge in your chosen field of study. You learn basic library techniques so you can find books, periodicals, and articles on your subject of research; you learn how to use the card catalog or, increasingly, how to use computerized listings or service for on-line searches. In some cases, you will learn to make use of the experts whose opinions form the books and articles you have read through interviews or other personal communications. Some instructors encourage students to use additional information-gathering techniques common to many disciplines, including surveys, opinion polls, observation, and more extensive interviewing.

No matter what the technique, the heart of "research" is "search"—to discover information and connections between various types of information, to synthesize your findings and, often, to draw inferences or conclusions from the evidence you have discovered. Sometimes that means bringing together seemingly contradictory findings; for example, a professor you interview about her field of expertise may refute a point you read about in a book or journal, or perhaps the information from a book that you have used as the "classic" study in a field will need to be supplemented with more recent journal articles. While this process may be a new challenge for you, it is an important part of developing your critical-thinking skills. Such reconciliation of conflicting views, of old and new information, is excellent preparation for the kind of synthesis and integration of ideas and material you will be expected to do in your future academic and professional work.

Often students find it hard to imagine that they are genuinely contributing to the field in which they are researching and writing, particularly in lower-division researched essays. They sense that their instructor's knowledge far exceeds what they could contribute. We do challenge this view—students' insights and discoveries add tremendously to the academic disciplines, particularly as they begin work in their major fields. And students do need to learn, in any case, to address writing to academic audiences. But we suggest that an opportunity to write for an audience outside the college classroom can offer some real advantages.

When you write for an audience that genuinely needs the information you are discovering and synthesizing, you will often find that you are more engaged in your work, more concerned with getting accurate and up-to-date information, and more concerned that your connections be logical and that your style be clear and precise. Why should this be so? Often when we can visualize a real reader or readers we can get started writing, keep writing, and polish the writing more easily; we know for whom we are writing and for what purpose; we have the task to inform or persuade rather than to "prove or improve," the purpose of many academic writing assignments.

In writing for readers outside the classroom, discipline, or campus communities, such as community groups or local government agencies, you also have the opportunity to write for a range of audiences, from the general public, to public officials, to funding officers who offer grants, to volunteers who staff nonprofit organizations, to constituents of nonprofit organizations. Each type of audience has certain expectations for the form and content of the writing. For example, a first-year student writing for a church-run homeless shelter discovered that a key problem for homeless people on government assistance is having a place to keep their money between checks, since they often lose their cash due to loss or mishap. The student called or visited every bank in the city to find out which ones offered free or low-cost checking accounts; then he drew up a concise information sheet listing the bank names, addresses including cross streets, and exact costs or requirements. Another student researched local ordinances and tenant-landlord law; he then wrote up a clear, informative, concise information sheet for the shelter to distribute to interested low-income renters.

Not only did the students provide a service; they also learned to meet very specific audience demands: the information they provided had to be logically organized and up-to-date; the language had to be clear and understandable without being patronizing. The format had to invite reading and be visually appealing. The students who investigated these issues and then wrote up their findings were able to use the research and writing skills they were developing in their courses; at the same time, they developed their stylistic range and ability to synthesize and emphasize important points.

RESEARCH AND DIRECT SERVICE

Some students prefer to do direct community work and to use their research papers as an opportunity to learn more about the larger context of their study-service connection. One student worked for a local humane society and then did a research paper on pet-assisted therapy. Another student placed with elders wrote a paper on the effects of gardens on nursing home residents. Still another got involved with an organization supporting recent immigrants and wrote his researched essay on the NAFTA treaty. What students and instructors alike have found is that when students can combine their direct service and their academic studies in this manner, the two activities enhance each other; the firsthand experience and observation stimulates the research; the research amplifies the students' understanding of the societal issues raised in community involvement.

ACTION RESEARCH

Another approach to research in conjunction with study-service connections is known as action research. The definitions for this term vary, but most participants agree that action research is an activity directed by the community and conducted through the cooperative efforts of the community and the college community as a mutually useful enterprise. The community in this case is not a laboratory for students, but a partner. The student learns, but also contributes to the community; the community receives a benefit, but also helps teach the student. The community indicates the research needs, and the student brings his or her basic research skills to bear on issues of community concern. The student can gather data, compile results, synthesize material, interpret data, and write up findings in a manner appropriate for the audience. Often non-profit groups will want to see fully documented and developed essays of the kind students turn in to their instructors; occasionally, the results can be written up in a different manner, as on a grant application or in a less formal but nevertheless scrupulously accurate form.

Action research involves researching and writing for change, often social change; a study of causes of homelessness, for example, or overuse of emergency care facilities for basic health care can help government, nonprofit, and funding groups define and ameliorate specific problems. Students can often pursue opportunities in the community that relate to their own academic or personal interests. Two students interested in environmental issues (one is now a geology-physics major) wrote a collaborative documented essay for the Sierra Club International Committee discussing reasons why the Philippines should develop a biomass energy program rather than a geothermal program. To write the essay, the students had to understand what both kinds of energy were. They had to look at a model of biomass energy developed in South America and then compare the climate, geography, and sociopolitical concerns of both countries. Then they had to develop a comparison-contrast that supported arguments and answered objections. Another student worked for the finance department of a local city government to research and write about the effects of a state proposition on cities. In another class, students conducted research on classroom size and surveyed teachers and members of the public for the state senate office of research.

Potential areas of action research are numerous; a few that have yielded rich opportunities for students and resources for communities include health, environment, children's and women's issues, education, economics and work, housing, public policy, local government, mental health issues, and international issues. On some campuses, an office of volunteer activities or community relations has listings of interested community groups or government agencies who want student researchers. But even if you have to do your own searching, you still have many resources; you can start by checking the phone book listing under "Social Service Organizations." Probably quite a number will be listed, so you can start cross-checking by your interest and perhaps by location, especially if you need to rely on public transportation. Consider local government agencies as well; a regional park district or city council, for example, may have ample opportunities for you to develop interesting and useful action research projects.

Once you have identified potential projects, start early: if you want to do a project that is part of your class work, you need to get going right away. Get in touch with two or three agencies, asking to speak with the director or community liaison and clearly stating your name, institution, and purpose in calling. Emphasize that you are interested in the agency and would like to work on some research that the agency may need. If the conversation seems promising, make an appointment for an interview (see the section entitled "Interviewing" in Chapter 2). At every stage of communication be persistent, because people at these agencies are extremely busy. Note that if you get hooked up with someone's voice mail it will save time to clearly state your name, purpose, and telephone number or a time you will call back or can be reached. Also, be consistent: promise only what you can do, and deliver it.

If you and an agency identify and outline a project, find out if the agency has library materials or resources where you can begin your search. Investigate any promising leads in the community: printed material, people to be interviewed, good places to do on-site interviewing, and the like. Often agencies find it helpful that students have access to the college library system; be sure to take advantage of your college's library holdings. Find out how recent the information needs to be. Remember that the usual rules of research apply: keep careful track of your sources, cite all materials, document carefully. Know when to summarize, when to paraphrase, when to quote directly. Find out the format needed for your Works Cited list and if an annotated bibliography would be useful. And don't forget the instructor! You are probably writing for both audiences; your instructor will probably want MLA or APA format for the paper regardless of the agency needs, so get this worked out ahead of time. Some students have found revising a researched essay to the specifications of a second audience to be an excellent means for developing their writing skills. If such an activity doesn't appeal to you and your instructor, find out if the agency leader will accept the same format your instructor desires, or vice versa. We have found that nonprofit groups generally appreciate the well-documented, traditional format of researched papers. And remember that research is a process; meet with the instructor and the agency leader as the draft is in progress to check on the direction of your research.

Action research can be the most engaging, absorbing, and useful writing you will ever do at college; writing for an audience that genuinely needs and wants the information you have discovered and written can help you to feel less like a student and more like a "real" writer.

CHAPTER 2

Mapping and Reflecting on Your Service Learning Project

Progress Update Sheet
Service Learning Evaluation Worksheet
Project Evaluation
REFLECTING ON YOUR SERVICE LEARNING EXPERIENCE
Reflection Worksheet

MAPPING AND REFLECTING ON YOUR COMMUNITY SERVICE WRITING PROJECT

The following worksheets will help you to define and map the process you use to produce your community service writing project. We also provide worksheets that encourage you to evaluate and reflect upon what you are learning about your own values, how you are developing critical thinking skills, and in what ways your service learning experiences are enriching your academic learning.

Student Interest Inventory

Brainstorm and freewrite some responses to the questions listed on the "Student Interest Inventory Worksheet"; then look for patterns. Do you see any connections, for example, between your academic interests and some of the issues in your community that concern you? For example, are you interested in biology or geography in your academic work and environmental issues in the local or global community? Political science and grass roots movements? Social welfare or sociology and homeless issues? Botany and local community gardens? Psychology and domestic-violence support organizations?

In some cases, you may find that your academic interests and community interests are related. In other cases, you may see work in the public arena as an opportunity to broaden your interests and experiences; a member of the Young Republicans working with an immigrant workers' group and a left-of-center activist doing field research for a conservative city government took advantage of opportunities that gave them a broader perspective on the issues at hand.

Ideally, you will find a wide range of opportunities for writing and research in the community in which you live or attend school. Your interests and the community's needs will dictate what kind of study-service connection you are able to pursue. If you have a campus public service center or volunteer office, it could provide you with good leads on places that could use your interest, energy, and expertise. If not, you could take the initiative, perhaps with instructor or peer guidance, in seeking out such opportunities. If work in local community agencies or groups is not feasible, you could still write about issues that matter to you, publishing your work in campus or local newspapers. You could write letters to local or national leaders, and you could sharpen your research skills by taking on some of the library or other research work for nonprofit groups whose mission you support.

Student Interest Inventory Worksheet

Review the following questions as you consider the kinds of writing assignments and study-service connections you might want to pursue:

1. What kinds of issues are you most interested in discussing? What do you like to read about?

2. What is your history of work, work-study, volunteer work, or involvement in public issues?

3. What kinds of academic courses are you interested in?

Student Interest Inventory Worksheet (*cont.*)

4. What are some of the issues or problems on your campus or in your local community, at school or at home, that concern you?

5. What are your hobbies or special skills?

6. What particular academic skills do you have or are you developing?

Approaches to Combining Service Learning with Writing

TYPES OF SERVICE LEARNING PROJECTS

Use this worksheet for preliminary information gathering.

Service Learning Projects Log

Letters

Some students choose to write expository or argumentative essays on issues of public concern for their community service writing projects. Such essays can be either letters to the editor or opinion pieces known as Op-Ed pieces, because they appear opposite the editorial page of the newspaper. Students who wish to explore public issues can investigate opportunities to do so in the campus or local newspapers.

Newspaper:

Address:

Service Learning Projects Log (*cont.*)

Direct Service

Other students either are already engaged in community work or would like to perform direct service or volunteer work other than writing as part of their community service writing project. They then write journals or reflective essays about the experience.

Organization:

Address:

Contact person and telephone #:

Type of work:

Community Service Writing

Through community service writing, students write on behalf of community or campus organizations drafting and writing articles, informational materials, and proposals for nonprofit groups or local government agencies. Typically, students will turn in such materials both to their instructor, as part of their course work, and to the agency or organization who requested the writing project.

Organization:

Address:

Contact person and telephone #:

Type of writing needed:

Guidelines for Student Writers

The following guidelines offer suggestions for how to approach your work with the contact person at the agency where you will be working.

1. When you call the contact person at the agency, identify yourself as a student working on a community service writing project and make an appointment for a meeting. If you are working in a group, schedule a time for the meeting when every group member can be present.

2. Your initial meeting with your contact person is very important. Use this meeting to learn exactly what will be expected of you.

    A. What kind of document is needed? Who will read it? How will it be used? How long should it be? What format will the piece take? Should it be submitted on a particular type of computer disk?

    B. How will you get the information you need—from your own experience, from your college library, from the agency's library, from interviews?

C. When should you show someone at the agency a draft of your work? When will the final copy be due? When will it be printed in its final form?

D. Request models of documents similar to what you are writing that have already been produced by the agency. Studying these models will give you a good sense of what is expected of you and will help you to shape your writing.

3. Show your work to your instructor and to your contact person at the agency at least a week before a final copy is due. Both your teacher and your contact person will be interested to hear what the other reader/critic had to say.

4. If your document is to be printed—if, for example, it is a newsletter article or brochure—be sure to ask for extra copies of your finished work for your instructor to keep as a model for subsequent groups of students, and also keep one for yourself.

Guidelines for Student Writers (*cont.*)

5. Be professional about your responsibility to the agency. If you should decide not to write for an agency with whom you have been in contact, let the agency know immediately so it can find another way to get the task completed. If you need more help or information than you had anticipated, call the agency as soon as possible. Do not do your work at the last minute or ask for an extension.

6. Remember that when you do a community service writing project, you are working in the "real world." Staff members at public service agencies are often overworked; they may not be able to return you calls promptly, or their deadlines may be different from those in your class. It will help if you can be flexible and persistent.

Proposal and Contract for
Community Service Writing Project

Student Name _____

Course Title _____ Instructor _____

Date of proposal:

Names of any peer group members: 1. _____

2. _____ 3. _____

Agency representative and contact telephone, if applicable:

Subject/topic for project:

Goals for project:

Proposal and Contract for
Community Service Writing Project (*cont.*)

Type of project:

Logistical constraints?

Brief outline of project:

Audience:

Time frame:

Schedule for peer group meetings:

Time needed for research:

Schedule of conferences on drafts:

With peers:

With instructor:

Proposal and Contract for
Community Service Writing Project (*cont.*)

With agency:

Format: turn in typed copy? computer disk? formatted copy?

Final project due on:

Proposal checked by: agency _____ instructor _____

Thinking about How Your Audience Shapes Your Writing

When you are most deeply involved in the act of writing you will not be as concerned with your message to your public audience as you are with discovering and clarifying your own thoughts. Essayist and fiction writer Ursula Le Guin gives us insight into the different ways that a writer thinks as he or she is creating: "Although most writing is done in solitude, I believe that it is done, like all the arts, for an audience. . . . While planning a work, the writer . . . often must think about readers. . . . But once you start writing, it is fatal to think about anything but the writing."

Writing is both a process of discovery and communication; it is a process with many steps. A writer's relationship to his or her subject and audience develops along the path to a completed piece of writing. While the creative aspect of writing is at the core of the process, the depth of your thinking and writing will be developed through learning to communicate with a variety of audiences for a variety of different purposes.

In the past you may have written for yourself in your journal, for peers in your school paper, or for friends, parents, and relatives by means of letters. Perhaps you have written for employers while searching for a job, requesting a raise or a transfer, or proposing a new idea. Undoubtedly, most of the serious writing you have done has been directed to the teachers in your classes. The worksheet that follows will help you to face the challenges of writing for a specific audience and to formulate specific strategies as you shape your writing for audiences in your community or on your campus.

Audience Assessment Worksheet

1. How large is my audience?

2. How diverse is my audience? What is its gender? age? economic, political, and social background? What distinguishes this audience as a group that I am writing to?

3. What values do I share with my audience?

4. How are my values different from those of my audience?

5. Will my audience be interested in my topic? Why?

6. How will learning about my topic benefit my audience?

7. How can I engage my reader's interest in my topic?

8. What background knowledge does my audience need in order to understand the issues covered in my paper? Will any technical or complex words or concepts need to be defined or explained?

9. Do I need to learn more to reach out to my audience effectively and to explain my topic more convincingly?

10. How can I anticipate the objections that my audience may have to my information, approach, or point of view?

Intercultural Issues

To be effective learners and contributors in communities within and beyond the campus, we need to recognize cultural diversity and acknowledge our own cultural, ethnic, class, and gender orientations. We need to understand that we are shaped by our experiences and that we generalize from those experiences to deal with life and with others. The assumptions, values, and biases we derive from our experiences can affect how we interpret the actions of others, as well as how we react ourselves.

Our cultures, values, beliefs, and customs are our ways of dealing with the world. To assume that our way is the only view, the only way of doing something, the only way people relate to each other, is to fall into an ethnocentric mode, a way of seeing and communicating with others that assumes our way is correct.

There are specific areas in which we need to consider the customs and values of people from cultures different from our own. First of all, consider the issue of personal space. In some cultures, sitting or standing within a few feet of someone is invading that person's space; in others, such a practice is considered the norm in given situations. To some people, direct eye contact is considered disrespectful; to others, avoiding eye contact is seen as evasive. In some cultures, smiling is considered friendly and appropriate; other cultures value the ability to control and avoid displaying one's emotions.

We can't give you a course in intercultural understanding in this brief outline, but we offer the following suggestions to help you to raise your awareness of intercultural issues and to help you use your service learning experiences to increase your knowledge and understanding. We also refer you to Patricia O'Connor's article and to the "Questions and Answers about Community Service Writing" in Chapter 1.

Journal Writing and Reflection
on Intercultural Issues

REFLECT:
- on your own ethnicity, race, cultural values, and beliefs
- on the ways in which you view difference or different people

WRITE:
- about your own orientation and view of the world
- your thoughts, observations, understanding of difference (see also Tim Stanton's article on journal writing in this chapter)
- as you work in the field, continue to reflect on and write about your interpersonal relations and any incidents that you find difficult to cope with or stimulating to think about; use your journal to reflect on these incidents

COMMUNICATE:
- with your instructor, your peers, your organization leader or liaison, about the issues, experiences, and observations that come up for you during your service learning

Challenges of Collaboration

Just as each individual develops his or her own writing process depending on the nature of a particular assignment, so too will each group shape an individual working process for a collaborative project. Before beginning a collaborative writing project, it is important to consider the challenges that your group is likely to face.

There are definite advantages to writing in a group. When people are working together on a project, the group can undertake a more complex problem because more inventive power and shared information are available to explore the issues and to find solutions. The group can also accomplish more because the amount of work can be divided, with each member completing those parts of the project that seem most interesting to him or her. When working on your own, getting started, getting stuck, and losing interest can be problems. In contrast, when you are working collaboratively, members of your group may motivate you and help you to focus and develop your ideas.

At the same time, group members will need to make some adjustments in their personal schedules so that regular meetings can be held. The group will have to develop a consistent approach to the assignment. While you will not be able to include everyone's ideas, as you arrive at a creative, flexible compromise, the best ideas will find their place in the finished project.

To succeed with the collaborative project, all group members will need to be prepared for every meeting. If in the past you have been likely to do most of a paper the night before it is due, in this writing situation your lack of ongoing preparedness will affect all of the members of your group. On the positive side, if you do have such a tendency to procrastinate, the group project may help you to keep on track and to work at a regular pace. The success of your project will reflect your group's effort.

Your working style will be affected in other ways. If you are not accustomed to making compromises, a collaborative project will challenge you to learn how to present your point of view to others and then listen to the group's decision on how to proceed. This process will help you to become more flexible. Those of you who are shy will need learn to feel more comfortable about expressing your point of view. If you are the type of person who tends to react defensively when other people give you advice, you will have the opportunity to try to distance yourself from your immediate personal reactions and try to listen objectively to others.

Another advantage of working together to develop a writing project is that from the very start you will be sharing your ideas and drafts, receiving immediate feedback on your writing, and working together to imagine the audiences for your completed project. While you will have to justify the decisions you make about including information and examples, or about your point of view, tone, and organization, defending your ideas and writing will help you to improve your part of the project.

Through the process of completing your collaborative writing you may realize that you have a particular skill that does not come easily to others in your group. Perhaps you are good at coming up with creative ideas or at doing close editing; maybe you have a well-developed vocabulary or are good at solving organizational or logical problems. Your classmates' appreciation of your special skills can certainly build your self-confidence. While some frustrating situations are inevitable when working on a collaborative writing project, what you will learn from your peers and the satisfaction you will feel when your project is complete will make it all worthwhile.

Collaboration Guidelines
Working with Peers

Students who aren't used to working on projects collaboratively may be apprehensive about peer group projects. Assignments up to the college level have generally been individually produced. But some college writing, and much writing in the worlds of work, is collaborative—people work together both in initiating and generating material and in composing and revising it. Some guidelines may prove useful for those students newly involved in collaboration.

1. However groups are formed—by putting together people who sit near each other in class, through assignment to projects, or through common interests in projects or topics—get the names, telephone numbers, and addresses of others in your group right away.

2. Share your schedules; write down times and days when everyone has free time or can make free time; check on evenings and weekends as well, but remember that if you work with community groups, some are open only traditional office hours, that is, weekdays from eight o'clock to five o'clock.

3. Find out if someone in the group has a car. If you work with a community group off campus, figure out how you will get there: walking, bicycle, public transportation, or private car.

4. If possible, assign a coordinator who will get in touch with everyone for work sessions, whether they take place in the community to gather information or on campus at the library for a writing or research session.

5. Make sure someone is responsible for collecting documents that the group produces, for copying materials for all group members, etc. While on the subject of photocopying—make sure someone doesn't get stuck with the copying or gas and parking expenses. Either share expenses, or ask your instructor or the agency about petty cash or access to copy machines so that you can reduce or eliminate out-of-pocket expenses.

6. Decide how you are going to allocate the work so that all in the group are equally responsible. For example, if you are writing a newsletter, you could divide up the articles. Everyone could type his or her own article; someone with page layout expertise could do the layout, someone else could proofread and edit, while a fourth could get the draft and then the finished document back to the community group. If the project is research-oriented, the group could divide up sources to investigate and then meet to share information and coordinate and select material to include. The point is to share the work and to share the learning experience.

7. Coordinate how the actual writing will be done. Some groups select chunks of a larger assignment for each to write and then work to blend the styles for consistency; some pairs have both members draft and then one revise and one edit. Some assignments lend themselves to clear division of tasks: for example, each student in a group of four wrote about one endangered species for a nature guide and handbook for a zoological society. Generally, collaborative work will receive one grade shared by all group members, so it is important to be fair and equitable in distributing the work.

Student to Student: Guidelines for Small Group Meetings
by Julie Phillips

When I was planning a group presentation with my classmates, staying on track turned out to be our biggest obstacle. We had a tendency to jump from one part of the presentation to another, without completing the organization of either. As soon as one of us took charge, however, we worked much more efficiently. We had sufficient creativity but were missing a leader.

From this experience, I learned that the most vital element of a productive group meeting is a strong leader. This person should not dictate what is to be done but should simply make sure the meeting is systematic and complete. If the meeting is directed down an efficient path, there is more time for the development of ideas and the refinement of details. This will all lead to a successful presentation.

Besides having a good leader, all members should know and understand the subject matter well. There is nothing worse than spending half an organizational meeting explaining the subject matter to an unprepared member of the group. Similarly, everyone should come with a few ideas in mind. Meetings can be much more efficient if they are focused on the collaboration and improvement of ideas rather than the generation of them.

The last thing to be considered during a group meeting is sensitivity to others. Constructive criticism should be both welcomed and given, but it is good to remember that people are sharing personal, creative ideas. If group members feel they could receive ridicule for their ideas, they might refrain from sharing their insights and some potentially excellent ideas could be needlessly lost.

Throughout the meeting, a few questions should be kept in mind to ensure an effective, interesting presentation:

1. Is the presentation going to be entertaining and hence effective? Will students be actively engaged in discussions and activities?
2. Is sufficient attention given to both activities *and* discussions?
3. Is there a balance between fun activities and work-oriented ones? Or could work-oriented ones be made into fun ones as well?
4. Is there enough time in the class for all planned activities? (If there's a possibility of a time shortage, decide which activity should be omitted.)
5. What is the learning value of planned activities? Could they be made more conducive to learning something new rather than reiterating previously known and understood subject matter?
6. Will discussion questions lead to further questions and thus create an animated class?
7. How do various ideas relate to the subject matter presented? Will students and instructors be aware of these connections?

Preparing for Conferences

While you may not be familiar with short student-teacher conferences, they can be very useful in a number of ways. The majority of our students rank conferencing as the best way of developing their writing and critical thinking skills. As instructors we have found that working individually with students provides the opportunity to guide a student's writing project in a way that is not possible through written comments or lecture formats. In conferences students and instructors can clarify misunderstandings and avert frustrations—thus, progress occurs more rapidly. Before you meet with your instructor prepare a list of specific questions or concerns that you would like to cover. The following list presents some ways in which conferences can help you with your writings.

Ways in Which Conferences Can Help with Your Writings

Conferences can help:

- To focus ideas and invent new ideas for future assignments
- To clarify your instructor's ideas and expectations through one-on-one dialogue
- To check that the paper has a clear overall purpose, that the paper is directed to its audience, and that all of the major points are clear
- To discuss the specific writing style required for your project, which may not be addressed in the classroom where more general writing issues and topics are explored
- To help you learn how to recognize your own mistakes in order to learn to revise more effectively
- To develop an understanding of the positive aspects of criticism and to lessen any defensiveness that you may feel about paper comments
- To guide you through a series of revisions with individualized attention
- To develop your self-confidence
- To examine new experiences or problematic situations related to your service learning project

Keeping a Journal

A writing journal can serve many functions in a writing course. It can help you in the process of discovery and reflection as a place to record ideas, insights, and freewriting on issues of interest. It can also be a reading journal where you record reactions to the course readings, with questions on texts, explication or analysis of texts, connections between readings, and other exercises to help you understand the readings and their connections to class work and experiences outside of class.

A journal can also serve as a logbook of your experiences. To integrate out-of-class experience into your course, your journal can include records of meetings with your instructor, with peer groups, and with organization leaders or people in the community. Keeping accurate accounts of your meetings will help you to stay on track and coordinate your work. It is especially useful to record dates of meetings, people present, delegation of responsibilities or tasks, goals, and finally a summary note of the meeting or telephone conversation.

In this type of experiential notebook, it is helpful to write an entry after every encounter in the field, every meeting, and every working session. Early entries could entail observation and description of the site in your community and the people you encounter. You might find it useful to include space in your logbook to write out your impressions of what you see, whom you deal with, and how you see your experience affecting you and your writing process.

As a research tool, the journal can help you as you sift through information and as you make sense of your findings: you can record your research notes on one side of a divided sheet of paper and reflections on the other, or you can record your notes on notecards or in computer files and use either a computer file or notebook for your reflective notes and freewriting about your topic.

Many students find that a journal gives them a place to write unedited, ungraded thoughts and ideas; such a space to write can help a writer develop a sense of personal voice as a writer. Students who are uncomfortable writing formal, graded essays may be surprised at how easily their writing can flow when they feel the freedom to write knowing that a critic or editor is not looking over their shoulder. If you can use such a space to develop ideas, to amplify thoughts, and to consider questions and answers, you may find it easier to select and develop certain ideas for graded essays.

Some instructors will want to evaluate a journal, especially if it represents a significant portion of the course. Often, though, the criteria for assessment of journals are less stringent than those for traditional essays.

The journal, whether formally assessed or simply considered a place for your own thoughts and feelings, can become the cornerstone of your writing course or an optional tool to help you think.

Suggestions for Journal Keeping

You may find it helpful to include the following points in your journal You can modify this model to meet your particular interests and project.

1. Your project as it is assigned

2. Your meetings and phone conversations with the agency people and your experiences working at the agency

3. Relationships that you see between course readings and experiences at your project placement

4. Ideas and information gathered that you can integrate into a research paper.

5. Questions, concerns, and insights that you have as you work with your agency and write up your project

6. An evaluation of what you are learning as you work through your project

Writing about Public Service Experience: The Critical Incident Journal[1]

Timothy K. Stanton

Many students keep journals in order to chronicle their life experience. If you keep such a journal, you probably record notes on the people around you, on the activities in which you engage, and on your personal feelings and reactions to it all. You probably select items to record from the myriad events in your day without much thought, perhaps unconsciously, according to your values, interests, or even whim.

The "critical incident" technique of journal writing is a more structured approach to writing about experience, which can be used to reflect upon, monitor, and evaluate community service. It differs from more traditional journal writing in many ways.

First, the critical incident journal writer consciously selects incidents to reflect on through writing based on the degree of impact they have on her reasons for engaging in service. Rather than a descriptive record of daily life, a critical incident journal includes detailed analysis of only those incidents which change you or your perspective on your service experience.

Second, critical incident journals contain reflections on incidents that are not necessarily treated in normal time sequence. Chronological time is not an important criteria for deciding which incidents to include in a journal and when to include them. The impact of incidents on you, even if you do not become aware of that impact until you experience several other incidents, is far more important.

The third and perhaps most important element in critical incident journal keeping is that the writer uses reflective analysis of selected incidents to measure the progress she makes toward her objectives as a volunteer. Rather than simply describing and interpreting an incident and the people involved, this reflection technique enables the writer to use the incident and its impact as a means for self-monitoring and personal exploration.

Obviously, in keeping this sort of record no two people will consider the same two incidents as critical. For example, a volunteer working in a youth agency may change her perception of herself, or of her service organization, or even of society as a result of an altercation with a particular youth, and thus wish to explore this incident in her journal. Yet, to another student the same confrontation could be a minor incident, having little personal or educational impact, and therefore not merit inclusion.

---

[1] Adapted from J. Flanagan, "The Critical Incident Technique," in *Psychological Bulletin*, July 1954, Vol. 51, No. 4, pp. 327–358; and from J. Duley, "Cross Cultural Field Study," in *Implementing Field Experience Education, New Directions for Higher Education*, No. 6, Summer 1974, pp. 13–22.

Whether you include an incident in your journal depends on how it relates to why you have chosen to engage in service and on what you are trying to get out of your volunteer experience. Consider yourself a ball rolling across a pool table. In a critical incident journal you will want to record and reflect upon the points of impact with other balls which cause you to change direction. You will want to describe both the incident of impact and how it affected your progress as a volunteer. At first it will be difficult to determine which incidents comprise these points of impact. However, as time goes on, you will become increasingly adept at recognizing a pattern in the kind of incidents which have a powerful effect on you. This understanding of your own patterns, alone, should prove useful in helping you make key decisions later on.

REFLECTION AND WRITING STEPS

1. Identify a critical incident and the issues involved with as much specificity as possible.
2. Describe the relevant details and circumstances surrounding the incident, so that you and any potential readers will understand what happened. (What? When? Where? How? Why?) Describe any people involved and their relationship to you and to each other. (Who?)
3. Describe your role in the incident—what you did, how you acted, how others reacted to you, etc.
4. Analyze the incident. How well or badly did you understand the situation? How did you handle it? What would you do in the same way or differently next time? Why? Remember to provide observational data to support your analysis.
5. Analyze this incident in terms of its impact on you and explain why you view it as critical. How does the incident relate to your reasons for engaging in community service? Has it stimulated you to change your objectives or change your views about service? What have you learned from this experience? How has your perspective on yourself been changed and/or reinforced? Where do you go from here?

In spite of the structured nature of this writing, your journal entries need not be long nor arduous. The importance of this exercise is learning to sift through your experience for what is important in terms of objectives you have set for yourself, and to evaluate your progress in a very subjective way. The goal is not to chronicle successful or catastrophic incidents in your service experience. Critical incident writing is an opportunity to learn and practice an effective reflection and monitoring process and to seriously explore yourself, your service experience, and your values and perspectives related to service.

One final word. Critical incident journal writing, like any sort of writing, can become a tedious chore of filling up space, or it can become an exciting record of your work and a reflective, dynamic exploration of yourself, your experience, and your views on issues related to your service. The difference has a lot to do with your attitude toward reflection and writing and the commitment you make to explore yourself and your experience. With a positive attitude and a firm commitment on your part, this form of writing can become an effective tool for furthering your development as a volunteer and as a person. When your writing serves you this way, it will become a rewarding and fulfilling experience.

Examples and Case Histories

Writers often support their basic ideas by drawing upon their personal experiences and observations and then developing them into examples or case histories. We all learn by watching, by listening, by doing. It is also important to reflect upon your experiences with and observations of your service learning as you have recorded it in your journal. In writing about your service learning experiences you may decide to include parts of a discussion that you had during your service experiences; descriptions of neighborhoods, classrooms, and community centers you have observed; and stories or anecdotes that clients have shared with you or that developed from experiences you have had. For example, Jonathan Kozol composes a portrait of a gifted inner-city teacher, "Corla Hawkins," (which is included in Chapter 3 of *Writing for Change*) as a narrative designed to support his main point that even in the worst schools there are exceptional teachers whose classes "stand out like little islands. . . ." The following guidelines present significant issues to consider when developing narratives that serve as examples or case histories.

Guidelines for Examples and Case Histories

1. Have you established a clear purpose for your case history or narrative example? Is this particular example designed to introduce a concept, to support a secondary point, to create an effective contrast, or to provide an effective conclusion?

2. Have you gathered enough details for your example or case history, using techniques such as freewriting, brainstorming, and reviewing on-site observations collected in your journal?

Guidelines for Examples and Case Histories (*cont.*)

3. If your narrative or extended example is based on your own observations, have you gone back to observe again, using your journal to record more details?

4. If your narrative or example is based on an experience that happened some time ago, have you tried doing some freewriting or brainstorming to help you to remember more about that period in your life?

5. Are your examples or case histories relevant to the main points you are making? Are they *typical* and *representative of* situations that happen regularly in the community in which you are working, or do they seem too unusual to stand as representative instances? If you have any doubts, you might share your examples with clients or supervisors in your service placement and ask them some of the questions above.

6. As you rewrite and polish: Have you been as specific as you can be, or do you need to use a dictionary to replace vague words with more specific and descriptive terms? Have you substituted more concrete verbs, nouns, and adjectives for more abstract ones? Have you captured concrete images?

7. As you continue to write and revise your paper: Have you weeded out details and incidents that seem to slow down your narrative, that don't relate to or help explain the main point of your article or essay?

8. Have you tried using some dialogue? Dialogue often brings a narrative to life. However, it is best to use dialogue sparingly; try to include just a few key lines from the people involved that will help to establish their characters or the nature of the conflict among them.

9. Have you used connecting words and phrases such as "then," "soon," "after a few minutes," "in a little while," or "the next day," in order to inform your readers that time is passing and that you have skipped over a certain amount of time because for a few minutes, hours, or even days, nothing relevant to your story or main point was happening?

10. As you rewrite, are you developing clear logical connections between all the events mentioned in the narrative so that it will be easy for your reader to follow?

Interviewing

You can gather primary source material yourself by interviewing people in the field, whether faculty experts on your campus, community leaders, or leaders of local nonprofit organizations.

Before an interview, gather as much information about your subject as possible. If you are interviewing a faculty expert on the subject of your research topic for a course, make sure you have read some general information about the topic and preferably several other sources on the subject. If you are interviewing someone in the community about his or her role, perhaps in a community agency or organization, gather as much information from other sources as possible in order to use your interview time efficiently. Generally, the interviewee is helping you, although he or she may have an interest in educating college students or in getting the word out about his or her community work.

If you are working on a project with peers, compose questions together and then select the best questions of the group. Consider your goals, the time constraints, and the availability of other sources before making the decision to request an interview.

Be polite but persistent in setting up an interview. It may, in this age of voice mail, take several attempts to get through; when you do leave a message, identify yourself, your institution, and the purpose of your call. Be clear about the amount of time you expect to need, but be reasonable about others' time demands. You can accomplish a lot in a ten- or fifteen-minute interview if you are well organized. Review your own schedule and peers' schedules to determine a number of possible time slots because you will have to work with the interviewee's schedule. Write down the time, date, and place, and give the individual your phone number in case there are last-minute conflicts which necessitate rescheduling the interview. Keep the interviewee's number with you as well in case you are delayed. If possible, bring a tape recorder to the interview so that you can obtain accurate quotes and information and so that you are free to concentrate on what the interviewee is saying; that way you can follow up interesting directions in the conversation without worrying about taking notes. You could, though, designate one or two note-takers if you are working in a peer group so that the other group members can pursue the conversation without attention to note-taking. Be sure to ask permission before you begin taping, and test the recorder before you rely on it.

Be on time for the interview. If you are a few minutes early, use the waiting time to observe the environment and review your questions. Be conscious and considerate of workers; often, community and nonprofit organizations have limited work space and privacy. When your interviewee is ready to talk with you, introduce yourself and any peers working with you. State the general purpose of your interview and proceed with the questions. Since time may be limited, you may want to start with some of the most important questions to make sure those questions are answered. When possible, state your questions positively: not "You don't serve a large population in this city, do you?" but "I understand that you serve some twenty percent of the city; has that population remained stable for the past five years?"

Pay attention to cues from the interviewee. If he or she has agreed to a specific amount of time, respect the time constraints. Though many people in managerial or academic positions send fairly clear end-of-interview signals when their time is limited, be alert to body language and other cues that indicate that the individual needs to close the interview. Thank him or her for the time and information as you depart, and remember to send a brief thank-you note as a courtesy.

Ask the interviewee's permission to use his or her direct quotes. Most will agree if you promise to quote them accurately and to avoid quoting them out of context. Remember the spirit and context in which the remarks were made, and don't use the interviewee's words in a manner that suggests something he or she did not say. It would be courteous, and sometimes is required, to send a draft of the interview or article to the interview subject to check the accuracy of the quotes or other information you obtained from the interview.

Interview Worksheet

1. How and why did you select the person you are interviewing?

2. How do you plan to conduct the interview? Will you ask the interviewee if you can tape your discussion or do you plan to take notes during the interview?

After the Interview

3. What is the approximate age, gender, education, and social, cultural, and family background of the interviewee? How might the person's background have influenced his or her point of view on the topic of the interview?

4. What were your expectations before the interview? What did you hope to learn?

5. Contrast your expectation of the interviewee's responses to his or her actual responses. Where did the interview lead you? Did it bring up new issues? Did it help you understand a part of your subject that you had found difficult or confusing? If you are going to write an article, remember to include some direct quotations from the interview as well as summary and paraphrase.

6. Did the interviewee suggest any solutions to the issue? Did the interview change your mind about any aspect of the issue that you are researching?

7. Did your interview encourage you to do more research? What type? What do you want to learn about your topic now?

8. How do you plan to incorporate the information gathered in this interview into the paper or article that you are writing?

Progress Update Worksheet

Your name:

Project title or brief description:

Agency/organization, if applicable:

Contact person:

Peer(s) in your group:

Brief outline of your project:

Your progress to date: What have you completed, what is in progress, what remains to be assigned or completed?

Have any problems surfaced? Describe:

Formulate a plan for dealing with problems or obstacles: What can you do? What resources, in people or material, do you need to complete your project?

What is your timeline? When are your deadlines? What needs to happen so that you can meet these deadlines?

Service Learning Evaluation Worksheet

1. In the short term, what immediate insights did you gain?

2. What insights are likely to come through sustained service and reflection?

3. What relationships did you find between your service experience and your academic course work?

4. If you were to serve as a mentor for a student beginning a community service writing project, how would you prepare the new student? What would you emphasize about the learning opportunities in a service project?

5. Did you learn more from expected opportunities (e.g., information shared by the agency) or from unanticipated opportunities (e.g., a chance conversation with people from a neighborhood or a client at a shelter)?

6. Do you think the placement at the agency where you worked could be built into a longer-term relationship? How might this happen? In what ways would your campus or department benefit? In what ways would the agency benefit?

7. Did your agency supervisor and instructor structure your service learning opportunity appropriately? Do you have any suggestions for ways that they might help to improve the placement and writing assignments so that future students will gain more from their service learning experiences?

8. After your placement, how do you differentiate between service that supports or facilitates learning and learning that supports service?

Service Learning Evaluation Worksheet (*cont.*)

9. In what ways was your study-service connection about "educating for a life of active citizenship"?

Project Evaluation

Name of agency: _____

Total # of students in your group (including yourself): _____

Title of your project: _____

1. Give a brief history or overview of your project: for example, what you wrote, the joys and trials of the project.

2. Do you feel that the piece you wrote will be useful to the organization? How?

3. What did you find most worthwhile about the project? Did it
provide you with new educational experiences? What did you learn
about writing that you might not have learned in a classroom?

4. How many meetings _____ and/or phone conversations

_____ did you have with your contact person?

Date draft turned in to instructor: _____

To contact person: _____

Date final copy turned in to instructor: _____

To contact person: _____

5. Do you have any advice or suggestions for how the Community
Service Writing Project might be improved?

Reflecting on Your
Service Learning Experience

Reflecting on what you learned is one of the most important goals of a service learning experience. You will develop your critical thinking skills as well as your capacity to be resourceful as you define, analyze, and interpret the new social experiences you have had working at a service agency. Your reflection should discuss the ways that your placement helped you to learn and to grow both emotionally and intellectually. As in the other stages of this project, develop an organizational framework that helps you to explore and keep track of your own thoughts and feelings about your project. The questions on the worksheet below should help you to understand and clarify what you have learned from your project.

Reflection Worksheet

1. How did this experience contrast with your previous classroom and writing experiences?

2. What did you learn about the importance of communicating with new audiences while completing this project?

3. What did you learn about working collaboratively? What insights have you developed about the value of discussing experiences, ideas, and strategies? If you produced a collaboratively written piece, what did you learn from this particular aspect of the project?

4. What did you learn about yourself—your personal values, your cultural values, your gender assumptions, and your expectations and responsibilities as a member of your campus and community and as a citizen of our country?

5. Did your understanding of how you learn change through your service experience? Why you value your education? What you expect from an educational experience?

6. What did you learn about the social issues that the agency was working to change and improve?

7. Did the reading and writing that you did for your class help you to understand the issues and the people you were working with at your agency? In what ways?

8. Would you choose to be involved in a study-service connection in the future? Explain your decision.

CHAPTER 3

Behind the Scenes: Building a Community Service Writing Project

The following two community service writing projects are presented with the writing activities that students completed to help them record, analyze, and later evaluate and reflect upon their service learning experiences. The first project was completed for an educational program at Stanford. The college students wrote and helped to produce their newsletter. This project is representative of a newsletter project that you might be asked to undertake for a nonprofit organization. The second casebook, based on the work that a group of four students did for the Patient Resource Center at the Stanford Hospital, represents a more complex placement project with a variety of writing and volunteer opportunities. We think you'll find that reading these casebooks will prepare and inspire you as you begin to work on the project that you have selected.

CASEBOOK 1

Reach Out Newsletter

Kathleen Chandler

Rich Crowe

Kwan Ping Chua

Jayme Plunkett

Ann Sheehy

Jeremy Taylor

THE COMMUNITY SERVICE WRITING PROJECT WITHIN THE SETTING OF THE COMPOSITION CLASS

The Community Service Writing Project for Reach Out* was completed by students in a first-year composition class that focused on the social issues theme "Writing for Change." Thematic issues in the students' reader included education and community, health and community, and nature and community. The service placements for this class were arranged to extend the themes; the placement for the education theme was at Reach Out, a program that helps high school students whose parents did not attend college to make a positive transition into college. The students in this eleven-week composition course were required to write four essays and complete one collaborative community service writing project, or they could have chosen to write five essays and not participate in a service learning project. Fifteen of the eighteen students in the course decided to work on community service projects. Six of the students chose to help produce the Reach Out Newsletter.

*Note: The names of the program, the program participants, and the program director have been changed to protect their privacy.

AGENCY PLACEMENT SHEET

Students were given the following placement sheet before meeting with their contact person. You will note that they had a number of different writing projects.

Placement Sheet

Reach Out
Local office: CERAS Hall
Stanford, CA

Purpose

Reach Out is a program designed to provide a variety
of academic support services to low-income and/or
first generation college-bound students. The program's goals are to motivate students to attend
college, to improve their academic preparation,
and to demystify the process of preparing for and
applying to college. During the academic year,
Reach Out students receive tutoring and college
counseling and participate in academic and career
workshops on Saturdays throughout the semester.

Writing Task

Write articles for the newsletter. Regular features
include profiles of students, profiles of tutors, and
program updates.

AN INTRODUCTION TO THE REACH OUT PROJECT:
By Ann Sheehy

Performing community service had been important to me throughout high school, and I wanted to continue to make it a priority in college. The following is a summary of my CSW experience. On the first day of the course, each of my classmates and I got to choose a public service organization to work with. I chose Reach Out, a federally funded program that provides a variety of academic support services to low-income and/or first generation college-bound students. Its purpose is to motivate and aid these high school students who might otherwise not attend college or even graduate from high school. In our program, eligible high school students from the local school district are matched with college tutors. Each Saturday, these tutors and tutee pairs meet for three hours to study high school course work, review for standardized tests, work on college applications, and basically create an outlet for support and friendship. During the 1992–93 school year in our local program seventy-five such pairs existed. Of those seventy-five, twenty-two were with high school seniors of whom 100 percent will graduate in June and go on to a two- or four-year university.

After selecting my placement, I got to work immediately! First, on the advice of my professor, I began to keep a journal of my community service experience. Then my group and I met with the woman in charge of the program who explained our project. We learned that we would each be writing a short article on an individually assigned topic. Each article would be submitted to the Reach Out newsletter which was to be distributed throughout the school district, around the campus, to the United States Department of Education in Washington, and to other private sponsors. Its purpose was to help create an awareness of what Reach Out is and to stimulate some financial support from the surrounding community.

Before we left the director's office, she gave us a brief history of the organization, some more specifics of our project, and the names of some additional people to contact to get more information. At this point, we were to gather information from these sources, write a draft of our article, and meet back with the director two weeks later on an individual basis. This process of gathering and revising was repeated (for me, three times!) until the final paper was produced.

JOURNAL: By Rich Crowe

Each of the six students kept a journal that included a record of their work on the project and what they were learning as they worked on their project. We have included Rich Crowe's journal:

Journal

Rich Crowe

Freshman English

Oct. 20
   I called my director at 4:45 P.M. and he was not
available. I left a message that I called, and said
that I would attempt to call him back tomorrow.

Oct. 21
   I called the director at 6:30 P.M. and the office
was closed. I left a message for him to return my
phone call on his answering machine with my phone
number.

Oct. 23
   I attempted to contact the director by phone at
12:45 P.M., and again he was not in. I left another
message asking for him to return my call with my phone
number.

Oct. 23
   The director returned my call at 2:00 P.M. and I
told him that I wanted to write for the Reach Out newsletter. He told me that I needed to contact the newsletter's office. The newsletter editor was going to be
out of town until Tuesday. The director said that he
will give her the message to call me when she gets back
into the office. He also said that if she does not
call me by Wednesday, I should contact her.

Oct. 30
   I called Reach Out at 1:30 P.M. and asked to speak
with Susan the editor. She was not available at that
time, so I left a message for her to call me with my
phone number. I am now beginning to get impatient,
since I would like to get the necessary information to
begin my writing project.

Nov. 1
   I called Susan at 1:00 P.M. and she was not in. I
left another message for her to return my phone call.

Nov. 3
   I phoned Reach Out at 11:45 A.M. and Susan was not
available. I again left a message for her to call me
back. I have talked to other students in our newsletter

group, and they have also had difficulties contacting Susan.

Nov. 4

I called Susan at 10:00 A.M. and she was not in. I again asked for her to return my call as soon as possible. It is apparent that Susan is difficult to get hold of. I have now tried calling her at numerous different times of day, but it has not seemed to work. I will continue calling and hopefully she will call me back.

Nov. 6

I phoned Susan at 9:30 A.M. and she was there. She asked me to meet with her at 10:00 A.M., so I did. At the meeting she explained to me what the Reach Out program is all about. She told me that all of last year's students are now going to college. She then gave me three choices to write about for the newsletter. They were:

1. Writing a profile of the senior class
2. Writing profiles of the teen counselors
3. Writing about Reach Out alumni

I chose to write about the alumni. I chose to write about Maria, who is in her second year at UCSB. Her phone number is (805) 968-6253. It is my job to interview her by telephone and write a short piece on her. I need a rough draft by Friday at 9:00 A.M., which is my next meeting with Susan. She also recommended that I focus the article on how well high school prepared Maria for college.

Nov. 8

I interviewed Maria by phone. I took notes of the conversation in shorthand in a notebook. I should be able to write my article from these notes, but I told Maria that I might need more information later and she said that it would be fine if I called back again. I thanked her for her time, and that was my first ever interview.

Nov. 13

I met with Susan at 9:00 A.M. and gave her a copy of my rough draft. She seemed to like it. She liked the points I made and the quotes I used to support them. Susan asked me to include one or two more sentences on being away from home and any advice for parents that

Maria might have. I agreed that this would make the article better, and I said that I would call Maria back to ask her the questions. That was the only change that Susan wanted me to make in the article. I am to bring in a copy of my final draft on Tuesday or Friday of next week along with my computer disk, which they will take the article from to set up the newsletter. I feel like I've actually written something worthwhile. I enjoy this type of writing much more than writing essays.

Nov. 14
   I called Maria at 12:45 P.M. and she was not in. She does not have an answering machine so I will call back later.
   I tried again at 3:30, but no one was home at that time either.
   At 8:30 P.M. I again tried and got in touch with Maria. I asked her the questions I needed to complete the article and told her how it was coming along. She seemed happy and asked me to tell Susan that she would like a copy of the finished newsletter.

Nov. 20
   I went to the Reach Out office at 10:00 A.M. and dropped off my article and my computer disk. I thanked them all for their time and they thanked me for writing the article. That was the end of my writing project.

THE REACH OUT NEWSLETTER

**REACH OUT
SENIOR PROFILES**

One Saturday, I had the opportunity to meet some of the high school seniors in the Reach Out program. When I arrived at the center, they were writing essays for college applications; when I left a few hours later, they were just on their way to individual three-hour study sessions with the tutors.

For three to five years these high school seniors have been spending their Saturdays and summers doing school work. Sound crazy? No. They're smart. Focused. Dedicated. Hard working. Determined . . . and totally inspirational.

Heather is a young woman with a plan for her future. She explained that she plans to be an elementary or junior high school counselor and eventually open her own practice. Currently, she is one of the Vice Principal's student assistants, and she works as a peer counselor to help kids at her school keep on track and stay in school by talking to them, calling them daily, and making sure they go to class and do their homework. In talking with Heather, it is clear that her gentle but commanding voice would make her a good counselor. Heather has been in Reach Out since the summer of her eighth grade year and says that it has "helped me out tremendously." She says that it is like an alternative to school, where you know all the kids and have counselors whenever you need them.

Dana goes to Woodside High School now, but she and her family have lived in many parts of the world. She was born in what is now Ho Chi Minh City, Vietnam. When she was four years old, she and her family moved to Indonesia, and one year later, they came to the United States. She has a great talent for languages and can speak Vietnamese, Chinese, and English, and she is learning Spanish in school. Dana wants to major in Business Administration in college. She wants a job where she can travel to other places and meet different people. Reach Out has helped Dana a lot, even though at times she says she's been exhausted from all the work. "They keep nagging you!" Now as she looks forward to college, Dana's happy she had the emotional and academic support from Reach Out. "I feel really comfortable with these people."

Alberto found out about Reach Out when a representative came to his junior high school. Meeting new people is one of the great things about this program for Alberto. And, like nearly all of the people I interviewed, his favorite part of being in Reach Out has been the summer school program. Every year since he was accepted into Reach Out, he has lived with his fellow students in the dorms for six weeks during the summer. He has taken a variety of classes ranging from math to ethnic studies. But Alberto's real love is music. One day he'd like to work as a DJ or technician or "just anything" at a radio station.

Rosa wants to be a civil engineer. In eighth grade her class went on a tour of the city and talked to the mayor, mainte-

nance workers, and a civil engineer. The engineer told them about a housing project that was about to be built on an old dump site. The project was eventually built, but Rosa says that even though it looks nice, she wouldn't like to live there. Now she's determined to do better. At her school, she takes part in a group called Math, Engineering, and Science Achievement (MESA). She has been in Reach Out for four years and says, "It's really good to come every Saturday and see the friends I haven't seen all week.

When I asked Patty if she was glad to have been involved in Reach Out for the past five years, she replied with a definite, "Oh yeah." She was soft-spoken and friendly, and said that Reach Out has helped her get good grades in high school. Reach Out tutors and counselors have answered her many questions, academic and beyond, about high school, college, and job opportunities. Patty speaks Spanish and English, studies French in high school, and is thinking about continuing her French studies in college. However, like most high school seniors and college freshmen, she hasn't decided in which field she might like to major in college.

"Reach Out is a great program," according to Jane, and she would recommend it to any high school student wanting to go to college. Jane goes to Kennedy High School and insists that she wouldn't be thinking about college if she hadn't gotten involved in Reach Out, although she adds that her mom has helped her a lot as well because she "pushes me all the time." Today, women in the police force are still not all that common, but Jane plans to beat the statistics. Her lifelong goal is to become a police officer.

Pilár is a high-energy young woman who is very involved in her high school and her church. She goes to a private school where she is one of only seven Latinos. As a cofounder of her high school's Multicultural Awareness club, she is part of a support group for minority students and their parents. The group provides tutoring and counseling, and helps recruit minority students to the school. She is also part of a church group that goes on retreats with high school kids who are having problems at home or in school. Pilár plans to work hard and take advantage of the opportunities that a college can offer by majoring in Human Biology or Pre Med. She also wants to try something new and take a Mexican Dance class (Ballet Folklorico).

These are only a few of the students of the 1992 Reach Out senior class. With just this small taste of the character of the students involved in Reach Out, I was taken by the energy and determination these high school students have. With the amount of time and energy Reach Out students put into their high school studies, it's no wonder that the program has a 100 percent college entrance rate.

(Stanford Freshman Community Service Writer: Kathleen B. Chandler)

SOUTHERN CALIFORNIA COLLEGE TRIP

On October 20, 1992, eighteen Reach Out seniors and two staff members set out on a trip that covered nearly seventeen hours of driving, ten hours of tours and discussions, and five different cities . . . all in a matter of four days. Why? Their goal was to visit five Southern California colleges, giving the students some firsthand experience of what each individual campus is like.

After leaving their host college, their first stop was the University of California at Santa Barbara (UCSB). From there, it was on to California State University at Long Beach (CSULB), San Diego State University (SDSU), the University of San Diego (USD), and Pomona

College. At each school, the students received a tour of the campus and were given a chance to ask questions.

The tour allows each student to gain their own perspectives about each college by talking with current college students and being able to see the campus itself, instead of just glancing through a college catalog. Jane, a third-year Reach Out student and a senior from Kennedy High school, said the tour influenced her decision to apply to one of the colleges that the group visited. Prior to her visit, she had no intention of applying to any Southern California schools.

The Southern California college tour is an excellent idea and offers students a great opportunity to learn firsthand what prospective colleges are like and whether or not the atmosphere is what they are looking for as a part of their college experience. It is the best alternative to college catalogs.

(Stanford Freshman Community Service Writer: Jayme Plunkett)

ALUMNI ADVICE

Maria C., a Stanford Reach Out alumna, has some advice for high school students. Maria is now in her second year of college at the University of California at Santa Barbara. She attended Sequoia High School for four years and was in the Reach Out program for the last three.

Maria started high school in the E.S.L. program, since her native language was Spanish. As a result of her language difficulties, she was placed in the low-level math classes in which she did not belong. Maria worked hard on her English skills and got A's in her math classes before she realized that she could get involved in her own education and change to more challenging classes. She got herself transferred into the more difficult math courses which helped her to be better prepared for college, where she plans to major in accounting. If Maria had not changed her classes, she may never have been in the position to major in accounting.

Stories like this one cause Maria to think that high schools could do a better job of preparing students for college. "High schools should be geared toward preparing students for college," says Maria. "Nowadays a high school education is not enough. The high school needs to prepare you for a college education." This is where the Reach Out program comes in. The program helps high school students prepare for college. Maria's advice for high school students is to stay in the RO program and not to fear college. She says, "Do not be afraid of the large college classrooms, the entrance exams, or the applications. Stay in the program and you'll be all right." Being away from home is another concern of many high school students. Maria made new friends at college by joining the STEP program (similar to the Bridge program) which she recommends. By making many friends she says, "you won't become as lonely or as homesick." Maria also recommends that "parents support their children's leaving home for college since it helps them become more mature adults." The moral of the story is to get involved in the education process which can start by joining Reach Out, and to see it through to a college education as Maria has.

(Stanford Freshman Community Service Writer: Rich Crowe)

POINT INCENTIVE SYSTEM

Free movie passes, $100 GAP gift certificates, Santa Cruz boardwalk passes? Wonder how *you* can win these prizes?

It's really easy through the Reach Out Point System! Initiated last year, the system was designed to monitor the extra incentive to work hard. Everything from telephone calls between tutor pairs

to actual attendance at Saturday sessions is recorded, and points are then awarded accordingly. Each tutor pair can earn a total of thirty points a week—ten for tutor/tutee communication and twenty for each Saturday morning session. Tutor coordinators may even award bonus points for perfect attendance, going to meetings, or other supplemental activities that teach students to be more accountable for their actions. The tutor pairs with the most points at the end of the year win incredible prizes!

But does the Point System work? According to Heather O., the students involved feel that they have been more motivated and excited since the program started. Heather, last year's second-place winner and four-year Reach Out student, thought that the program increased motivation for those students who may not have kept in close contact with their tutor otherwise. The prizes, she said, are "an extra boost!" And this year, that boost is even greater—with the cooperation of many local businesses, even *more* great prizes will be offered!

So, lift your expectations and meet the challenges of the Reach Out Point System—what do you have to lose when there's so much to gain?

(Stanford Freshman Community Service Writer: Ann Sheehy)

REACH OUT THROUGH ACADEMIC YEAR PROGRAMS

Hey you! Now that I have your attention, do you know why high school students from East Palo Alto come to Stanford on Saturdays? Is it to watch the football game between the Cardinals and the Nerds from UC Berkeley or is it to catch the Stanford Women's Volleyball team in action? Of course not! They come to Stanford to "Reach Out."

Reach Out is a national academic program targeted at high school students who are first generation college-bound or who come from low-income families. The program's goal is to help these high school students academically and to prepare them for college. Seventy students are currently participating in the program and more than 90 percent of these students will eventually enter college.

Reach Out achieves its aim by organizing and coordinating various academic and counseling programs. The most important one is the Academic Year Program that has an intensive academic focus all year round. This program is designed to assess the individual student's academic needs, to assist the student's progress in class, and to provide the student with necessary information concerning the college application processes.

The program is divided into different sections to meet the specific needs of different classes of students. Freshmen are enrolled in the Study Skills class while Sophomores are enrolled in the College Exploration class. The purpose of the Study Skills class is to help ninth graders make the transition into high school. The purpose of the College Exploration class is to expose Sophomores to the many different college systems and to help them to select high school classes on the basis of college requirements for admission. Juniors are enrolled in an intensive test preparation class which emphasizes verbal drills, as many of the students are not native speakers of English. A typical lesson includes doing comprehension exercises and learning new words to help expand the students' vocabulary.

In their senior year, Reach Out students have many opportunities to talk with the project director about their thoughts of going to college and any other questions or concerns they might have concerning college life, which usually includes sharing their apprehension about going away from home to college, as well as selecting colleges and majors.

Seniors also receive help in completing the cumbersome college applications, financial aid applications, and housing forms. A crash course in writing is also organized for the Seniors to help prepare them for college application essays. Furthermore, Seniors are counseled about what colleges to attend after they have received responses from the various admissions offices.

Another way Reach Out assists the students academically is to conduct tutoring sessions every Saturday from 12 P.M. to 3 P.M.. Each student has an individual tutor to help him/her with the subjects in which he/she needs help. The tutors are Stanford students who volunteer three hours every Saturday for an entire academic year. The tutors also serve as mentors and counselors to the students. In addition, exciting field trips to various college campuses and places of social, cultural, and recreational value are planned for the students regularly.

Rosa, a senior at Sequoia, has been with Reach Out since her freshman year in high school when her brother introduced her to the program. She is receiving tutoring in English and Math which she finds "very useful." The tutoring sessions also help her "not to get behind in class." As a senior in high school, she finds the SAT Prep Class especially beneficial as it provides her with practice tests and testing strategies. Rosa believes that Reach Out is a "worthwhile program" and she is "very glad to join it."

Reach Out has helped hundreds of first generation college-bound high school students perform better academically and thus has increased their chances to enter college. If you are also a first generation college-bound student in need of advice about college and help with school work, get an application now and complete it today.

(Stanford Freshman Community Service Writer: Kwan Ping Chua)

EVALUATING THE REACH OUT PROJECT:
By Kwan Ping Chua

The following student evaluation will help you to understand the learning process, the challenges, and the rewards of this particular community service writing project:

When I requested a Freshman English track with a community service writing program I hoped to be involved in some community work besides writing for the various organizations. I was very excited when I learned that I had been placed in such a track, and I looked forward to volunteering my time to do some community service. On the third week of class, my professor showed us the list of agencies that were participating in the CSW program. I decided to get involved in Reach Out, a federally funded program that helps first generation college-bound high school students, because I was interested in working with teenagers. However, I was disappointed when I went for my first meeting with the Assistant Director of the program. I found out that I would be writing an article for their newsletter and would not be actually participating in any community work. Nevertheless, I was still enthusiastic about writing the article as that would be my first time writing for a real audience instead of writing only for my class instructor.

My first meeting with the project director went smoothly. She showed me a list of topics to write about for the newsletter; I chose the Academic Year Program as I was interested in the ways that Reach Out had been helping the students. I was feeling very excited at the prospect of my article appearing in a newsletter. We decided to meet later in the week to discuss more about my assignment. Meanwhile, she gave me a copy of the latest newsletter and some brochures to read. Reading the articles in the newsletter was especially helpful; I developed insight into the style and tone to use when writing the article. I realized that most of the articles were written in an enthusiastic tone that portrayed Reach Out as a program filled with fun and excitement. Furthermore, reading the articles kindled a burning desire within me to start writing immediately. Unfortunately, I had to wait a few days for my second meeting with Susan to get more information.

My second meeting with Susan was also a successful one. We had an interesting conversation as well as an informal interview. She gave me a lot of information on the Academic Year Program to help me get started with my article. In addition, she suggested that I contact one of the participants in the program in order to get a different perspective on the program. I got the contact number of Rosa, a senior from Sequoia High School, whom I planned to call that night.

After the meeting, I rushed back to my room to write the article. However, writing the article was not as easy as I thought it would be. I was unaccustomed to writing for a real audience, and it was difficult starting the article. Only after reading through the articles in the previous newsletters did I manage to write the introduction. I tried to convey enthusiasm to the readers through the use of short sentences; furthermore, I tried to use simple language as English is not the native language of most of the readers of Reach Out's newsletter. My writing process was slow and tedious, as I had to stop constantly to think of ways to make the article more interesting.

Besides the difficulty in writing the article, I was also frustrated with Susan when she did not turn up for the third meeting. I tried calling her many times after that but she was always not around. It was after a week that I managed to get her. Unfortunately, we could not agree on a time to meet. Finally, I decided to leave my first draft in her office for her to go over. During the week, I tried calling Susan to find out if she had finished looking through my draft but I was always unsuccessful. Just before Thanksgiving, I managed to contact her and she promised to give me back my draft before the Thanksgiving break. I completed my article over the Thanksgiving break, and I gave it to Susan on the first day of December. She seemed to be impressed with it and even commented that it would appear on the front page of the newsletter. Although I was really excited about that, I was more relieved that the project was completed as it was both time-consuming and frustrating to work with Reach Out.

Looking back at my involvement in the project, I realized that although I was not actively involved in community work, writing an article for Reach Out's newsletter has enabled me to understand the work that goes on behind the scenes in a community service organization. I began to understand that it was often not Susan's fault when she couldn't make it for an appointment; most of the time, she was too busy or her attention was needed in some other more urgent matters. Besides coordinating the program, she also has to write proposals to improve the program, advise the students when they have difficulties, and bring the students for field trips to various universities in California; I began to sympathize with her.

Perhaps the greatest joy in participating in the community service writing program is to know that Susan, along with her staff, really appreciated my time and my effort to help lighten their loads. It is comforting to know that the article will be published in the newsletter and will serve as another way of reaching out to those students that are in need of academic help and advice but are unaware of Reach Out's program. I believe that I have benefited more from the community service project than I have contributed to Reach Out. It has been a learning experience working on "a real-world project," writing for real audiences, and interacting with other people who have different viewpoints. I certainly look forward to another quarter of involvement in the community service writing program.

CLOSING ADVICE, STUDENT TO STUDENT: By Ann Sheehy

When I was done, I had a chance to reflect on my community service writing experience. Performing community service almost always produces a feeling of well-being—helping to write the Reach Out newsletter was no exception. I share the following tips, based on my experience, that I think will help you to meet the challenges of your service learning experience:

1. Always keep in mind the audience who will be reading your writing.

I had always written essays to be read and graded by a professor, but with my CSW project, I had to grab the attention of parents, students, and teachers in the Sequoia school district as well as the Stanford community. Though it is hard to write for a different audience, this aspect of the project helped me develop and expand my writing skills.

2. Keep a journal.

I recorded every phone call, appointment, frustration, and excitement I experienced through the course of my project. This not only helped me to stay organized, but it helped me to evaluate my experience after I had finished.

3. Realize that a community service writing project is more difficult than an ordinary essay.

When writing a research paper, it is easy to open a book to find information whenever you need to. With CSW, you may call an important information source only to find that they are out of town for the week! Missed meetings, numerous phone calls, and multiple revisions are all inherent in this type of writing project. Try your best not to get discouraged.

4. Start early!

(See above!) The "Night Before" plan just won't work in CSW!

5. Most importantly, keep in mind that your work is valuable.

My experience with Reach Out taught me so much about what actually goes on "behind the scenes" at community service organizations. I saw how much work, dedication, and determination goes into making a public service organization run smoothly, and how much of that burden is laid on a disproportionately small number of people. This made me realize that yes, Reach Out really *did* need our help, as we were helping, in however small a way, to lighten the organization's enormous workload. This realization helped make the frustrating times a little easier.

Our group was glad we had the opportunity to work together on the newsletter. As classmate Jeremy Taylor summarized, "This project gave purpose to my writing and introduced me to something new and challenging."

AGENCY'S EVALUATION: By Arnolfo Merced

I just want to go on record in praise of the experience Reach Out has had with the real writers. I participate in the program because I enjoy working with the students and strongly believe that students are provided with an educational experience unlike that in an average undergraduate course. I must also admit that Reach Out really benefits from the writing assistance the students provide.

I usually assign newsletter articles which consist of student profiles, program descriptions, staff interviews, and general press releases about up-to-the-minute events. I give real writers options: I allow them to choose the article they want to pursue. I love sitting with them and playing the editor looking for various angles to the same story. Quite frankly, it's fun!

My approach is simple: Real writers call and I set up a meeting with them as a group. I provide them with an overview of the program, its mission, participants, and successes. This usually hooks them. They then select their topics and make an individual appointment with me to discuss the specifics of their assignments. If a real writer's assignment is to interview a Reach Out student, I will issue a phone number and invite the writer to a tutoring session or Saturday College where he or she can meet with the person. I also make it a point to meet with each real writer prior to first and final draft deadlines to review his or her work and answer program-related or technical questions.

One of the reasons that Reach Out might be so popular as a community sponsor is that the students not only learn about the writing process, voice, and audience, but they see in flesh and blood the subjects they are writing about. That is to say, Reach Out comprises individuals working collectively in various components of the program toward a common goal: to prepare and motivate low-income high school students for college. And each real writer, as part of a collective, is researching and writing about one piece of this large puzzle that is then given shape

in the form of a newsletter. This, I believe, moti-
vates a real writer to write for Reach Out.

   I would love to answer any questions you have about
community service writing and Reach Out. Feel free to
call me at anytime.

Sincerely,

Arnolfo
Program Director

INSTRUCTOR'S EVALUATION

The Reach Out placement has always been one that I can depend on. Because the office is on campus, and I have worked with the directors in previous quarters, I had a good sense of what types of writing they would expect from students and how they would work with them. I think the directors do an excellent job of setting up a positive collaborative relationship among the students. I believe that having established a relationship with an agency before sending students to work at that agency can be a crucial factor in a project's success. While new placements are certainly worth undertaking, they do involve more time and more risk.

   The six students who worked on this newsletter were motivated to learn more about the lives of the high school students and share their new insights in the articles they wrote for the Reach Out newsletter. The students matured through the process of working together and with the agency. In addition, all of the students felt challenged by having to write for a new audience. They shaped their writing with their audience's backgrounds and interests in mind. Their "worldviews" were broadened by finding out more about the Reach Out program and the students who participate in the program. Most of all the students realized that what they were doing was genuinely appreciated and useful to the overworked staff at Reach Out. Many of these students went on to volunteer at other nonprofit organizations on and off campus.

CASEBOOK 2

The Patient Resource Center at the Stanford Hospital

Rosa Contreras

Isela Franco

David Hollander

Melinda Lorensen

THE COMMUNITY SERVICE WRITING PROJECT WITHIN THE SETTING OF THE COMPOSITION CLASS

The Community Service Writing Project for the Patient Resource Center at the Stanford Hospital was completed by students in a first-year composition class that focused on the social issues theme "Writing for Change." Thematic issues in the students' reader included education and community, health and community, and nature and community. The service placements for this class were arranged to extend the themes; the placement that developed the health theme was at the Patient Resource Center, an organization which provides support services for cancer patients at the Stanford Hospital. The students in this eleven-week course were required to write four essays and complete one collaborative community service writing project, or they could have chosen to write five essays and not to participate in a service learning project. Fifteen of the eighteen students in the course decided to work on community service projects. Of these fifteen, four wanted to work at the Patient Resource Center. Each of these students told their instructor and Pat Fobair, the Director of the Patient Resource Center, that they chose this placement because one of their grandparents or close friends had had cancer or had passed away after struggling against cancer. Two of the students were also interested in majoring in pre-medicine and continued to work at the Patient Resource Center after their writing course was completed.

AGENCY PLACEMENT SHEET

Students were given the following placement sheet before meeting with their contact person, Pat Fobair. You will note that initially they had a number of different writing and editing options from which to choose.

```
"Surviving!" Newsletter
HO103 Patient Resource Center
Radiation Therapy Unit
Stanford University Hospital
Contact Person: Pat Fobair, Clinical Social Worker
```

Purpose:

"Surviving!" is a newsletter written and created by cancer patients for the benefit of cancer patients and their friends and families. Our goal is to share common experiences and to help recovering patients manage the challenges of their illness, treatment, and life after cancer. The editorial board welcomes letters from readers about common concerns and issues present in the newsletter. We also welcome poetry, artwork, or any information you would like to share which would be of interest to our audience.

Writing Opportunities

Attend editorial board meetings:

- Review stories printed so far, select best of stories for a book.
- Write your own personal reflections on personal experience with cancer in family, friends, or self.
- Continue helping board pull a book together.

While the students were working for the *Surviving!* newsletter, their primary focus was helping to evaluate materials that had already been published in the newsletter for a book that the group hopes to publish. Only one student in this group actually wrote a piece for the newsletter. After meeting with Pat Fobair, the four students—David Hollander, Isela Franco, Rosa Contreras, and Melinda Lorensen—completed a Project Proposal Contract. (A copy of this form is included in Chapter 3 of this guide.) The students also submitted a narrative summary of their project and goals to their instructor, which is printed below. Comparing the agency placement sheet and the proposal, you will see that the project that the students and the agency supervisor Pat Fobair agreed upon reflected the needs of the agency and the interests of the students. The proposal was written by Melinda.

STUDENTS' PROJECT PROPOSAL: By Melinda Lorensen

The contact person we met with was Pat Fobair. She asked us to compile a list of articles from the *Surviving!* newsletter, a quarterly publication that is distributed to 2000 people. She gave us over 100 articles to read. The newsletter's goal is to provide cancer patients and their families with an opportunity to express their emotions and frustrations with combating the disease. We were asked to read through the quarterly issues from Fall 1987 to Fall 1992 to try to decide which of the articles in the newsletter would appeal to people our age. The long-term goal of the project is to select articles and create a book which will serve as a unified source for cancer patients, their friends, and their families. After finishing our individual lists, we agreed to compile them into a "master" list of articles that we liked. The editors of the *Surviving!* newsletter will use our list as a guide for choosing articles for the upcoming book. This is our major assignment.

David, Isela, Rosa, and I are also expected to write a collaborative article that describes our project for the next issue of the newsletter. In this piece we will describe our role as part of the community service writing project and our role as part of the book project for the Patient Resource Center.

No one else in our group wanted to write a personal story. They felt that they were not ready to share their feelings—understandably, of course—about their experiences with cancer, but I decided to do so. My poems about my grandmother will be published in the next issue of the newsletter.

THE JOURNAL: By Isela Franco

After their initial meeting with Pat Fobair, each of the students kept a journal that included a record of their work on the project: reading the newsletter articles and organizing their prioritized list of the articles for readability that were categorized according to themes that included "Discovery," "Treatment," "Recovery," and "Progression." Students also reflected on what they were learning as they worked with people at the Patient Resource Center. Isela's journal follows:

> January 10, 1992. Friday. Went to visit Patricia
> Fobair at Stanford University Hospital. While I waited
> for her, I looked at various pamphlets that she had. I
> found it quite interesting. My thoughts kept going
> back to my grandmother, who died of cancer when I was
> in the fifth grade. I also kept thinking of my mother,
> who had a tumor just recently, but luckily it was
> benign. What struck me the most was a poem by an
> Albert Vilareal, age 19. I thought that it was very
> possible for my sisters, brother, and/or myself to have
> or get cancer. I don't know how I would react if that

were to happen. Mrs. Fobair told us what she wants us
to do, which is basically read numerous issues of
"Surviving!" and pick the ones we feel are the most
powerful. We also have to see if it is possible to
make a book and if it can be divided into chapters and
if so how. After our talk, Mrs. Fobair gave us a mini-
tour of the cancer/radiology department. She took us
into a room where a linear accelerator is found. I
think she said it was used to kill off the cancerous
cells. When I walked into that room, I felt nauseous.
It looked so scary and intimidating. I also saw a
booth used for bone marrow transplants. I can't
believe what people must go through just because of
cancer. No one should have to go through that horrid
experience!

January 23, 1992. Thursday. Today I read through half
of the newsletters. Most of the stories seem to convey
a message of hope and strength to the reader. Most
of them were about a person's battle with cancer and
their recovery or regression from the disease. I was
amazed at the courage that the writers had in just
being able to retell and, therefore, sort of relive
their experience with cancer. Although the overall
themes of the stories and poems was optimism, I still
found it depressing to read them. I can only imagine
what people with cancer go through, and I salute them
for their bravery in facing that dreaded disease.

January 24, 1992. Friday. Met with Patricia Fobair at
1 P.M. Melinda, David, and I told Pat Fobair what we
had already accomplished, which was basically read
through some of the newsletters. We compared the
stories we had already read to see if we had placed
them in the same categories. David's and my list did
not agree. By the end of this short meeting, about 20
minutes, we decided that by next Friday, we should have
read all the newsletters and categorized the stories.

January 30, 1992. Thursday. Today I finished reading
the rest of the newsletters. Although I still found
reading the newsletters depressing I felt satisfaction
in reading them; a satisfaction in knowing that there
is a strong chance of survival for most people with
cancer. Reading the stories also gave me a sense of
fear because although cancer can be beaten, I hope and

pray that no more members of my family should get the
disease. Also, I realized that I should do things such
as check for lumps on my chest frequently, and have
pelvic exams annually. Actually, all people should
check for early signs of cancer, and this will give
them a better chance of surviving.

January 31, 1992. Friday. Met with Pat Fobair at
1:30 P.M. We went through all our lists. Mrs. Fobair
compared them to see which stories we had the same.
She also went through the newsletters to actually
see which stories and poems we picked out. Whenever
she saw that we chose one of the authors that she
personally knew, she became excited. She was thrilled
that we picked some of the stories of people she knew.
I think that she really appreciated the job that we
did. We decided that by the next meeting, we would
have a composite list of the readings for her.

February 21, 1992. Friday. This was a really quick
meeting with Pat Fobair. It was only about 10 minutes
and I really didn't have to show up. I could have been
sleeping. All that happened was that David gave Mrs.
Fobair the final list of all the stories and poems we
liked. David then informed Mrs. Fobair of the idea for
all four of us in the group to write a story about our
experience in working with the Patient Resource Center.
She really liked and agreed with the idea. We decided
to meet one last time for a late lunch to turn in the
letter on March 6, at 1:30 P.M.

March 5, 1992. Thursday. Met with Melinda, David, and
Rosa to write the article for "Surviving!" I think that
the collaborative writing assignment went very well.
Input from everyone made the assignment go very fast.
I really liked and felt comfortable writing with the
group. There were a few times when jokes would be
made, and they were quite funny. I think that we
succeeded in making the paper general enough so that it
reflects each and every person's experiences and ideas
in the group. Before the project, I wasn't really sure
how the collaborative writing assignment would work out.
Actually, I was quite pessimistic. I thought that it
was going to be difficult writing with people that I
really didn't know. I wasn't really looking forward to

the experience. But now that it is done, I enjoyed it.
It was not as bad as I thought it would be.

March 6, 1992. Friday. Last meeting with Pat Fobair.
Met with her at 2:00 P.M. I went with Rosa in her car,
and we were late because we had difficulties parking.
The actual meeting went very well. I felt a sense of
accomplishment and perhaps relief at having completed
the project. Pat Fobair and three other staff members
of "Surviving!" whom we met today, seemed very pleased
with our work. They were grateful for our work and
our input on the newsletter and book. Coming out of
this meeting, I really felt satisfied with the project.
I felt that every member in our group did the same
amount of hard work in getting the project completed.
Although at times I did feel that the project was a lot
of extra work, like when we had to read all those
newsletters, I am glad that I chose this project. I
got to work with a very enthusiastic person, Pat
Fobair, and I learned more about what people with
cancer go through. I know I cannot possibly imagine
everything that a cancer patient goes through, but I
can now better understand their situation and ways in
which to help them.

Volume VII, No. 3

July/August 92

A CANCER PATIENT NEWSLETTER

Surviving!

Publisher
Department of Radiation Oncology
Stanford University Medical Center

Executive Editor Pat Fobair

Managing Editor Behrooz Ghamari

Art Director Wendy Traber

Editorial Board Pat Fobair,
Behrooz Ghamari, Susan Taylor,
Wendy Traber, Susan Weisberg

Staff Support Pat Fobair, Susan Weisberg,
Eamonn Dunphy, MD

Administrative Support
Susan Taylor

WHAT TO TELL YOUR CHILDREN WHEN YOU HAVE CANCER

by Gayle S. Tucker*

I was diagnosed with non-Hodgkin's lymphoma this past May. I'm 34 years old, have a wonderful husband, a great career, a son age four an a daughter age two and my world had come apart.

After a week of hospitalization that included my first dose of chemotherapy I had months of outpatient treatment ahead of me. The shock, terror and disbelief gave way to depression, fear, scans and treatment cycles. My biggest concern of course was what to tell my children. I would lose my hair, might be sick, would definitely be tired, would be home from work a lot, might have to be hospitalized again and the biggest might—death.

When I grew up I remember my mother and grandmother talking about people with cancer, saying they got the "Big C" or got the "Real McCoy." The media is full of details of famous people who die of cancer and my own best friend died of cancer at age 27. What else could I think other than I will surely die too. I was suddenly in a world I wanted nothing to do with. It was full of technical information, tests, blood counts, side effects, and many sleepless nights. There were days that I couldn't look at my children without getting hysterical crying. There were days when I felt like buying them each a present for the next 18 years so they'd have birthday gifts from me when I was gone.

I began to search for books about how mothers with young children coped with cancer. I couldn't find very much and decided on my own to be as honest as possible and to use my instincts.

I explained that I was taking medicine that would make my hair fall out and that I would wear a wig. I wore it out, but went bald in the house. It never phased them. Children are very accepting. I often wore bandannas through the summer and once came upstairs to find my husband had put one on each child. We all had a great laugh. I had two wigs and was doing the dishes one night and heard two children hysterically laughing coming down the steps. They each had on a wig.

Luckily, I did very well on chemotherapy and never experienced the terrible side effects you hear about. My children continued their regular day care schedule and one of their teachers brought them home and helped me around the house on the weeks I received chemo. I was on a once every three week cycle. I continued to work and tried to keep things pretty much normal. The kids watched my husband give me a shot every night for 10 days following chemo to keep my white blood cell count up. They waited in line to get their pretend shots after me. I had to get and still continue to get gallium scans. I am injected with radioactive isotopes and can't pick up the children for about a week after the test. This is very difficult for convenience sake and also for love's sake. I just explain to my son that I have medicine inside of me so I can't pick him up or hug him. Every day for the week he asks "can you hug me tomorrow?" It breaks my heart, but is soon forgotten when the week is up.

After chemo I had 17 radiation treatments. Since I work part time my children had to go with me the days I didn't work. They watched the technicians place me on the table and then watched me from outside the room on a special TV monitor. My son thought it was so "neat." I always acted like going for radiation was just another part of our day together.

I never actually used the word cancer to describe what I had to my son. A mother of a friend of his at day care was treated for breast cancer during my treatment. One day he said to me "Jason's mom has cancer like you." He also surprised me once by using the name of the hospital where I was being treated and the name of my doctor. Children are very perceptive and he must have overheard my telephone conversations. I explained to my son that yes I did have cancer and was now all better.

I'm through with all my treatment and have been in remission since September. My hair has grown back. I have five years of scans and tests ahead of me and luckily an excellent prognosis.

More than half the people who are diagnosed with all types of cancer live. I think the emphasis in this country and in the media should be placed on stories of survivors. I still get scared a lot and worry about the future, but my children have given me great strength. I have to act normal and happy and function daily because of them. Even though I may be hysterical on the inside, on the outside all must seem OK. When I go for monthly check ups, I

continued on page 103

FROM THE EDITOR

This issue honors family members in support of the cancer patient. Family members, spouses and friends are the unsung heroes in the melodrama of the cancer-treatment experience. Studies by Cassileth (1985)* and others tell us that family members often sharethe same degree of depression the patient experiences.

We have been reviewing some data collected among patients with Hodgkin's disease during the early 1980s. Many of you participated in these studies. One recent result was that the mood and self esteem of 61 patients with Hodgkin's disease was better at the end of treatment when there was better family cohesion, less family conflict and more family expressiveness at the beginning of treatment.

Noticing that some cancer survivors experience physiologic or emotional distress after treatment, we wanted to examine various factors to see if we could explain why some patients did better than others. First, we located fourteen variables (like "extent of treatment," "body image," "energy loss") to see which factors most highly correlated with depression, psychological distress and self esteem among 403 patients who had been treated for Hodgkin's disease 1 to 21 years earlier (9 years later on average).

In addition to better family cohesion and less conflict, the factors most likely associated with better mood and self esteem were better energy, greater sense of control, and a better body image.

Next, we looked at 61 patients and compared their answers at three months during therapy and at twelve months after therapy was over. The patients who were happiest in mood and self esteem at the end of treatment were those who suffered less family conflict and enjoyed greater family expressiveness at the beginning of treatment. Having had less treatment and having greater sense of control over life were also predictive of mood outcome.

We can conclude that while there are many important factors to one's adjustment after treatment, including medical and physical variables, the family support was the most important. Patients with better family support showed less mood disturbance and better self esteem. Family support was the buffer against the major stress of having cancer. These results support our efforts to maintain or improve our relationships with family members and encourage individual and group programs for patients going through treatment.

Patients know who to thank when the experience is all over. When we asked the 403 Hodgkin's disease patients, "What have been the source of your greatest help during the cancer experience?" 60% said family and friends.

At the end the editorial board of Surviving! wishes to thank you and to congratulate you on your group responsiveness to our request that if everyone contributed their $12.00, we wouldn't have a deficit. During the last few months 93 of you sent us $2,517.00 contributing greatly to an improved financial picture. Thank you and please continue. We want you to remain on our mailing list and help keep the interaction going.

* Cassileth, B. R., Lusk, E.J., Strouse, T.B., Miller, D.S, Brown, L.L., Cross, P.A., "A Psychological Analysis of Cancer Ptients and Their Next of Kin." *Cancer*, 55: 72-76, 1985

THE ADVENTURES OF CAPTAIN CHEMO!   *by Barbara J. Schrading*

Cartoon characters named Captain Chemo, Good E-Cell, Bad Cell, and Dr. Pain are unlikely to make the general public smile. They won't compete with Dick Tracy, Nancy and Doonesbury. But cancer patients are intimately acquainted with the realities these characters represent. The patients in my support group with whom I shared these cartoons smiled and laughed and began to look forward to each "new edition."

"The Adventures of Captain Chemo" were created by my 23-year-old son, Eric, to cheer me as I began the battle against bone marrow cancer. The cartoon characters emerged first on the margins of letters. Later, they visited in full page, six panel cartoons.

Twelve days after I entered the hospital with severe back pains, the diagnosis was in. Multiple myeloma, cancer of the bone marrow, had caused damage to my bones leading to the fractures which caused my pain. My youngest son, Eric, had driven up the day before from Virginia Tech where he was a graduate student in wildlife biology. He was in my room when the doctor came in.

Eric held my hand tightly as the oncologist told me that the biopsy from the bone marrow he had taken a couple days before had shown lots of malignant plasma cells. This was a systemic disease. There was no cure, but it did respond well to chemotherapy. I could expect to get the disease in remission after up to a year of chemotherapy.

Cancer, the dread diagnosis. Chemotherapy, the dread treatment. I had heard stories about the side effects of chemotherapy which made the patient wonder if this treatment was worth it to get better. Nausea, hair falling out, fatigue. But we listened carefully as the doctor told us that side effects could be minimized. Treatment should start right away. I was moved the next day to the oncology floor of the hospital to begin chemotherapy.

Sharing hugs and tears and talk with my husband and three sons, I knew I had lots of support from them. They would help me get better. Eric had to go back to Virginia, but he promised to call and write often.

Just a week later, I met another ally in my battle with cancer. "Captain Chemo" was introduced in a marginal drawing on Eric's first letter. He created Captain Chemotherapy, a super-hero like cartoon character, who would help mobilize my body, represented by "Good E-Cell" against the ugly bad cells which threatened me. In the first cartoon, Captain Chemo "zapped" the bad cell which was producing excess

calcium. In the next letter he whacked him again, sending him away on a stretcher. At Halloween, Good E-Cell tricked "Bad Cell" into pulling a rope which dropped 10,000 tons of chemotherapy on his head.

I shared the smiles and laughter which this wonderful new friend brought with the hospital staff and with my visitors. Captain Chemo helped me think of chemotherapy as my friend and ally. Captain Chemo stayed close by posted on the wall by my bed and later at home on the refrigerator door.

As I began working with a physical therapist to walk again, under Captain Chemo's supervision, Good E-Cell was starting to bury Bad Cell, do his exercises, and lose his hair. He remarked, with a satisfied look, "I may not have hair, but I'm starting to feel better."

A month later, in the first full page cartoon, Pain Man tried to subdue Good E-Cell. But Captain Chemo set Good E-Cell on his feet and sent him to "deck" Pain Man. Gradually my pain did diminish. My bottles of various pain medications retreated to the closet shelf and Pain Man has not been back in the cartoons.

In his calls, Eric questioned me about my treatment, how I was responding, what else I was doing, whether I was getting out. He encouraged me to rest,

exercise, and take care of myself, and also to get out in the world again. The cartoons acquired a six panel format, a title, "More Adventures of Captain Chemo" and the addition of color.

After I joined a cancer patients's support group, I took my favorite Captain Chemo to one meeting. It shows Captain Chemo and Good E-Cell jogging together. As they rest on a hillside, hands behind their heads, Captain Chemo says, "of course it's going to be hard work, but with exercise and sleep, you'll be feeling a lot better and together we can really do a lot." As

they jog again Captain Chemo continues, "but you have to understand. . .," when he is interrupted by a surprise attack by Bad Cell. The always reliable Captain Chemo whacks him away, returns to put his arm around Good E-Cell and continues, "It's going to be a never-ending battle, but I'll be here by your side to help."

The other patients loved the cartoon and asked me to bring copies whenever I had a new "edition." They looked forward to Captain Chemo's further adventures.

By summer, thanks to chemotherapy,

good care, the love of my family and friends, rest, good food, laughter, faith, and whatever else contributes to healing, I was living a nearly normal life again. We were able to go on vacation to our favorite place, a beach cottage on Martha's Vineyard. All our family joined us—sons, daughter-in-law, grandson, mother, and . . . yes, Captain Chemo. One day Eric, surprisingly, stayed back from a trip to the beach. The next day the reason was apparent. He brought out the Captain Chemo T-shirt he had painted. The Captain Chemo "logo" was painted on the front. On the back, with his arm around Good E-Cell, the triumphant Captain Chemo held the ugly green Bad Cell upside down by his feet. We all celebrated!

Twelve months of chemotherapy ended in August. I had responded to treatment. The myeloma was in remission. I was on my feet again. My discomfort was minimal. The side effects of chemotherapy had been fairly mild. I even had a reasonable amount of hair left.

I would not miss the monthly treatments, but I would miss the good cheer brought by Eric's cartoons about Captain Chemo. Meanwhile, my doctor discussed a fairly new treatment used as maintenance therapy with myeloma patients with good results. The new therapy was alpha interferon. I would need to learn to give myself injections.

I had been on interferon treatment for a week when a letter came from Eric. Inside was a new "Adventures of Captain Chemo." Captain Chemo was telling Good E-Cell about a friend he wanted him to meet. Into the picture, riding on a hypodermic needle came this new friend, Interferon Man, ready to join the battle. "This is the person I wanted you to meet," says Captain Chemo. "This is Interferon Man." "Nice to meet you. I hope I can help," says Interferon Man.

I hope so too, and I look forward to more cartoon adventures representing the love of a son whose creativity has been a source of great strength in time of trouble. Δ

What to Tell Your. . .

take my children with me because it helps me to remain calm.

I pray that I will live to see my children grow up. Most of all I think my children are fortunate to have mother who will survive cancer. They will grow up and won't have to totally freak out when they hear someone has cancer or heaven forbid get cancer themselves. Hopefully, they can reassure someone in the future who faces cancer that people actually survive treatment and live on. They will hopefully never have to experience the terror I felt at hearing the word cancer because cancer does not have to mean death.

My advice to mothers with small children is to be honest, include your

children in your treatment. Cancer becomes a part of your life and will be a apart of mine for a long time. Having my children there beside me gives me the courage and reason for making that extra effort every day to go on and to be positive about my future. I can't wait until they're grown up to see what they remember and how they describe the experience to me. Δ

* Gayle Tucker was diagnosed with B-Cell lymphoma May 22, 1991. She has been in remission since September 17, 1991. She had a mediastinal mass diagnosed by a chest X-ray after she had developed superior vena cava syndrome, which she thought was a sinus infection. She was treated with six cycles of CHOPP and 17 radiation treatments.

MY MOM IS SICK

by Judith Strasser

I'm Fran. I'm seven years old, and my brother Andy is four. We live with our cat, Shadow, twelve fish, our dad, and our mom. But our mom is very sick.

What she has isn't like the flu, or even chickenpox. Our mom has cancer. It goes on for a long time, but she doesn't have to stay in bed.

Sometimes she feels pretty good. She takes us ice skating, or to the zoo. It seems like she isn't even sick, and I think everything will be OK.

But when she feels bad, I get very scared.

Once, she went to a hospital in a city far away. Our dad went too, to keep her company. Pops and Grandma came to stay with Andy and me.

Pops tells awful jokes. Grandma bakes cookies all the time. But Andy and I wanted our mom and dad.

I cuddled Shadow. Andy cuddled everyone (except the fish). Mom sent us a postcard from the hospital, and after two weeks she came home with dad. Pops and Grandma went back to their house.

But things were different here.

Mom couldn't pick up heavy things. Andy climbed on her lap. I scrunched beside her on the couch. She still read us books, but she couldn't swing us around like airplanes any more.

Mom slept late. Dad got up extra early to make us breakfast and pack my lunch for school. He gave me two cookies for dessert almost every day. Mom used to forget to give me even one.

When my mom got sick, I thought I might get sick, too. But mom says you can't catch cancer from someone else, like you catch a cold.

She told Andy and me what's going on inside her that makes her sick. She said that every person is made up of trillions of cells—tiny things you need a microscope to see. Cells divide to make more cells. That's how children grow. Cells divide in grownups, too, to make new hair, and fingernails, and skin.

But sometimes, something goes wrong. Some cells divide too fast, and they won't stop dividing. The person has cancer. That's what happened to our mom. Now her good cells have to fight the fast-dividing bad cells. I hope the good cells win.

Mom takes medicine to kill the bad cells. She goes to the hospital for radiation, too. The medicine makes her feel terrible, but the radiation doesn't hurt. It's like X-rays Andy got when he broke his arm. Mom calls it "getting zapped."

Mom's medicine made her hair fall out. She wears a scarf or a wig so people can't tell she's bald. I ask her to wear the wig when my friends come to our house.

Andy and I like to play doctor with our friends. We pretend Shadow has cancer, and we zap her bad cells with pretend X-rays and pretend medicine.

Andy wants to play dress up with mom's wig and scarf. Mom said maybe we can have them for our dress-up drawer when her hair grows back.

I asked mom, "When your hair grows back, will you be well again?" Mom said no. It will be a long time before we know if she is cured. She might get better, but she might not. I don't want her to die. I don't even like to think she might.

Most of the time, I don't think about it. Right now she's alive, and loving us. And that's what counts. ∆

Book Review

Friends Till the End

by Todd Strasser
Laurel-Leaf Books, Published by Dell Publishing, 1981

by Michael Ikehara

Defending a soccer goal, dating one of the most popular girls in high school and improving his grades were the foremost concerns for high school senior David Gilbert. Developing a friendship with the new student Howie Jamison was one of the last things on David's mind especially when Howie seemed so different and out of place. Howie was eager to make new friends and would talk to David at the bus stop. David only saw Howie during the first week of school and then Howie wasn't at the bus stop. David thought that Howie had just made some new friends and was catching a ride to school with them. It wasn't until about two weeks later that David found out Howie had been

TURNING POINTS: GLIMPSES THROUGH THE MIND'S EYE

by Kelly Marrapodi-Munsell

•**1979** When we were about 12 years old, my twin sister Tricia and I were at a softball picnic/celebration; our team came in first place for the season. While sipping on a diet grape soda (then sweetened with saccharin), I vaguely remember somebody coming up to me and saying, "You shouldn't drink a lot of that soda. It'll give you cancer." Ten years later, those words echo in my head and that scene is as vivid in my mind's eye as if it took place yesterday afternoon.

•**1979** On Thanksgiving Day of that same year, my uncle and his daughter came over for dinner. While my cousin was styling my hair, we were watching MTV. Olivia Newton-John's video,

"Heart Attack," was on. My uncle asked, "What is she singing about? A heart attack?" Then he smiled and piped up, "Next thing you know, she'll be singing about cancer." I was weak. I laughed myself silly.

•**Midnight, 1985** HAPPY NEW YEAR!! HAPPY NEW YEAR!! Here's to 1986. Let it be a GREAT year. A happy, healthy new year. Little did we know, neither a happy nor healthy new year was meant to be.

•**January 1986** My mother, 42, was four months into a battle with breast cancer that abruptly ended her life on December 1, 1986. She was misdiagnosed, and died at age 44. Her suffering and death was, by far, the worst thing

that's ever happened to me.

•**May 1986** My father underwent triple-bypass heart surgery.

•**June 4, 1986** Tricia and I, 17, graduated from Sahuaro High School. It was an awesome night!

•**Two Weeks Later** I woke up and noticed that the left side of my neck was swollen. I thought that I pulled a muscle. A biopsy the next day confirmed the doctors' belief—Hodgkin's disease—cancer of lymph system. Pretty unbelievable, I thought, for a person who never smoked, drank, or had a sick day in her life. After three surgeries and four brutal months of daily radiation therapy . . .

•**May 3, 1991** . . . Here I am at 2:40 a.m. reflecting, and thanking God for my four-and-half years of remission. I feel like the luckiest person in the world. "If you were lucky," says my father, "you would have never gotten cancer in the first place."

•**Turning Point @ age 22** 1991 has been, by far, the best year of my life. Although I'll never stop grieving for my mother, I have come to terms with my own cancer. I no longer live in fear of recurrence.

On December 21, 1991, Tricia and I graduated from the University of Arizona with degrees in education.

On December 22, 1991, I married Burr Munsell, the most wonderful, caring man I have ever met.

•**The Future:** Like everybody else, I don't know what the future holds— GOOD things, I hope!—but I am looking forward to it. What did I learn from my experience with cancer? It made me realize how very precious life is, not to take anything for granted, and to enjoy each and every day because it truly is a gift. I never thought I'd ever reach this point in my life. It's wonderful and I'm forever grateful.

Believe that you are going to make it. Whether you are fighting cancer or are into remission, take each day one step at a time. Be good to yourself, and be patient. Realize how very special you are and believe that you <u>will</u> be all right.

Celebrate. . . Life! Δ

---

hospitalized. Howie had been diagnosed with leukemia.

In *Friends Till the End,* author Todd Strasser, addresses the subject of adolescent cancer. Most children and adolescents rarely think about or discuss the subject of cancer unless someone in their family has had it. Strasser shows the evolution of David and Howie from being naive to knowing and understanding the consequences of the disease and its treatment. As David's understanding of cancer grows so too does his friendship with and concern for Howie.

The main context of *Friends Till the End* rarely discusses leukemia but instead focuses on the interactions the two teenagers have with each others. David's family and friends have a difficult time understanding his growing friendship with Howie. At first even David doesn't understand. His maturity grows as he learns more about leukemia and gets to know Howie better. As David questions how and why a young person can be afflicted with cancer, he comes to know what is important in life. David's mother is the most understanding of his new growth but his father has

a more difficult time with it. David's father wants him to become a professional soccer player but a year later, David had decided for himself to become a doctor. At Howie's home, his parents were, naturally, concerned about their son. His mother had the most profound change. She became very overprotective and worried and would become angry at those who did not share her feelings. But without realizing it, her attitude had a negative effect on Howie by fueling the fire of fear and guilt.

Strasser's fast moving novel effectively shows how adolescent cancer affects family and friends. Very young cancer patients seldom fully understand what is happening to them and adults usually become more aware of cancer the older they become. It is interesting and informative to see cancer from a young adult's point of view. Δ

Editor's Note:
Late Bill Soiffer's first battle with cancer inspired Ted Strasser to write this book.

Surviving

TOUCHING OTHER PEOPLE'S LIVES

by Joe Marcus

In April of 1990, when I was twenty years old, I was diagnosed with acute myelocytic leukemia. I was twenty years old. I was a young, active, hard working nice guy who had a love for life and a love for for children. None of this changed, of course, but for some time I would need everyone I knew and even people I didn't know to make me smile. Life is about laughs; about making people smile.

I entered Presbyterian Medical Center in Philadelphia, Pennsylvania, where I underwent induction chemotherapy. Chemotherapy is no fun; I wish that no one would have to go through it. But going through chemotherapy is often the only choice for some cancers. You have to fight fire with fire. I decided I was going to make the best of it. If you tackle anything in your life and do your best, you always come out a better person.

I stayed in the hospital for nine and a half weeks. During that time I underwent two cycles of chemotherapy drugs. These drugs in my system caused me to be very sick. I was sick all the time. But the most important thing is it was killing the leukemia. During my stay, we talked about plans for having a bone marrow transplantation. This would raise my chance of staying in remission and being cured. One month after I entered the hospital I was considered in remission. However, I would spend another month there due to complications.

I was released from the hospital on June 15, 1990. By that time I had lost a lot of my hair, but not all of it. The next two months I did a lot of eating. I gained back thirty pounds that I had lost during my hospitalization. During the summer of 1990 plans were arranged for me to be admitted to Johns Hopkins Hospital in Baltimore—known as one of the top hospitals in the world for bone marrow transplantation. If I was going to have a transplant, it was going to be at the best place possible for me.

When I entered Johns Hopkins on August 13, 1990, I had many tests done. A week later I had my bone marrow harvested (removed) from my hips. I was my own donor—it's called an autologous bone marrow transplant. My own marrow was removed, treated with high dose chemotherapy, too strong for the body to withstand, and then injected back into my body. At the time of injection, my immune system was already wiped out by less toxic chemotherapy drugs than the ones used to treat the marrow. The new treated marrow finds its way around the body and you have a new "baby" immune system. Well, it would be nice if all that could happen without complications. It doesn't. With no immune system, the body cannot fight off infection. For four months after my transplant I stayed in the hospital and for the majority of that time in my bed. I don't think any experience I've ever had or will have will come close to my experience with leukemia. I made it to where I am today.

Everything turned out great in the end. My transplant was successful. I live my life like I did before I got leukemia. People often ask me if I live life differently now. I tell them not really. I always believed. I believed when I was sick and I believe now. I enjoy children now as I always have. I like to make people smile and laugh; I always have. I like to touch other people's lives. I guess you can say I enjoy people even more now. So maybe I did change. I'm thankful for modern medicine, but it's more than that that saved me. It was the love and support I received from my family and friends and the belief I had in myself that made the difference. There are a lot of people out there who don't have that support. A large number of them are children; children who should be laughing and playing with their friends; they should be growing up. They need to believe in themselves and in their chances of becoming healthy again. They are just as sick as I was. They need people to make them laugh and smile.

Last year I began to give back. I rode in the Leukemia Society's Cycling for a Cure. I rode 25 miles just four months after I was discharged for Johns Hopkins. I raised $1,100 for needed research in finding a cure for leukemia. Leukemia really is closer to a cure than ever. I am the proof. I really am the proof. Last year I was the top non-corporate fund-raiser. I was third against the corporate sponsors. People are in my situation every single day. Because I am here to tell my story, I must work so that others may tell us their story. "When there's help, there's hope." Δ

YOUNGSTERS IN BATTLE TO SURVIVE

by Andrew H. Malcolm

At first, they sound just like teenagers—the awkward pauses to insure that they don't say the wrong thing, the almost palpable social discomfort, the exaggerated concern over blending with others, the "awesomes," the "uhms" and the "I mean likes."

But then, in conversations, something doesn't quite ring adolescent. These young people seem too wise, too weary, too wary. At a time when they should be concerned with pimples, pencils and passing passions centered on the latest unshaven, shirt-free rock band requiring mass adulation, these boys and girls know far too much about Vincristine, Cytoxan, Methotrexate, Adriamycin and Cis-platinum. They talk with the scarred openness of war-worn veterans twice their age about losing friends, limbs and battles.

In other words, these young people know cancer.

* * *

Every year 11,000 Americans under 20 are diagnosed with some form of the dread disease. Once upon a time, no one of any age escaped alive. A generation ago the C-word, usually whispered out of respect for the soon—to-be-dead, was a sentence of doom with no appeal. Today, 8 million Americans live with a personal history of cancer. Nearly 200,000 of them are young people.

Recently, about 50 of them from two disparate states gathered here for an evening of chatter, dancing, lasagna and chatter.

It's one measure of medical progress that two-thirds of all young people diagnosed with cancer now survive at least five years. That's a hard-won, tear-stained, nausea-filled victory for their patients, their families and the dedicated professionals who see them come and go from the oncology wards.

But how do adolescents who've confronted the end of life before their voices change, and then undergone chemotherapy, amputation, radiation and isolation, suddenly fit back into a teen society consumed with Friday's game, Saturday's mall reconnaissance and whether their high-tops are properly untied? How do bald 15-year-olds wearing wigs confide their fears about sudden aches to former friends who think remission has something to do with puberty?

> Sometimes everything gets pretty intense. You think about dying. But you can't talk with healthy people. They don't want to think about death, let alone talk.
>
> *Tom Roberts, a 17-year-old from Clarksburg, N.J.*

They don't.

Enter New Jersey's New Visions and South Carolina's Lasting Impressions. They're support groups for teens with cancer. In regular meetings at New Brunswick's Robert Wood Johnson University Hospital and Columbia's Richland Memorial Hospital, members talk with peers who've endured just about every cancer treatment.

"It's really neat," says Susan Lipani, who is 17 and a new New Jersey member. "There's like a special bond between everyone. You can talk about anything." At New Visions, Susan meets other young people who laugh with her at how hair grows back a different color or like baby fuzz, even the second time. They don't deem it strange when Susan always wears her Mets hat indoors. And they tell her cool stuff like how Gatorade reduces chemotherapy nausea.

"Also," added 16-year-old Kyra O'Hea of East Brunswick, "you feel like you're helping others." That can be uplifting after 18 months of chemotherapy and radiation as you await the installation of a new hip.

"Sometimes," said Tom Roberts, a 17-year-old from Clarksburg, N.J., who takes powerful pills daily, intravenous medicine monthly and gets a spinal tap quarterly, "everything gets pretty intense. You think about dying. But you can't talk with healthy people. They don't want to think about death, let alone talk. I had to give up soccer. New Visions is like instant deep friends."

* * *

The groups raise money for camps and trips. They write newsletters. They phone the relapsed or deliver balloons. They also visit the newly diagnosed as living proof of life. "We're survivors," says Tracy Scripko, the president of New Visions. "Cancer helps you find your true friends."

The other night cancer forged new friendships as the New Visions kids gave a dance for their Carolina peers. Some wore baseball hats or bandanas, even a helmet. There were crutches and prostheses along with the seeming sunburn and indelible purple markings that tell of targeted radiation. There was also dancing for the able, pool for those in wheelchairs, fried chicken for all and endless giggles and chatter.

On his first trip north, 13-year-old Ronnie Robinson learned that his were not the first fingernails to turn purple in the fight against cancer. Shannon Carmichael, who is 15, never thought of New Jersey children so sick that they, too, fell to 81 pounds. Mindy Davidson, who's 18, taught some guys the Electric Slide, the hot-test dance down South. There were even whispers of budding romance or two.

New Visions is planning a trip to South Carolina nest year, a division in time that healthy people can often take for granted. But Tracy Scripko has a different perspective. "I count my remission years like lucky stars," she says. △

form *The New York Times*, January 31, 1992

'WHO KNOWS? YOU COULD OUTLIVE YOUR DOCTOR'

by Brian F. Hayes *(Part II)*

ONCE AGAIN, I RETURNED to Dartmouth shortly after my treatments ended. On the surface, I had fully recovered; the rosy tint had returned to my cheeks and my hair was rapidly filling in. Inside, however, I was falling apart. During treatment, I was always surrounded by people who knew what I was going through. At school, I was alone with my disease, and aware that another relapse would likely kill me. But most of all, after watching my friend Ron die from a fungal infection, I realized that optimism alone is not necessarily enough to beat cancer.

I did not tell my classmates about my disease. I thought that keeping it a secret would allow me to fit in with my peers better and make it easier for me to forget about it myself. I could not have been more wrong.

At weekend parties, I half-heartedly joined my friends as they gyrated to deafening music, but I would inevitably find myself wondering, "How can I celebrate and act as if everything is O.K. when I don't even know if I will live long enough to graduate?"

I began to avoid parties, and instead threw myself into my studies and my work with the school newspaper. No matter how busy I stayed, however, my mind raced with thoughts of a relapse as soon as my head hit the pillow at night.

Through the winter of 1989, the isolation grew worse and the pressure of trying to live two lives began to show. I became depressed and I had difficulty concentrating. With midterms approaching, I seriously considered dropping out of classes.

Finally one bitter February night I snapped. The trigger was innocuous enough. A problem had made me miss a date with some friends. Instead of just shrugging it off, I exploded, snarling and cursing at everyone around me. That night, my friend and classmate Roger Freeman, one of the few people who knew what I was going through, took me aside. We talked most of the night, about life, our goals and priorities and how we would accomplish them. Somehow during that long talk, Roger convinced me that, although I didn't have control over how long my life would be, I could have control over the quality of it.

Roger was right, of course. I had been allowing the disease to run my life. With his encouragement, my thoughts shifted away from thinking about the "what ifs." From that point on, my emotional health improved. Most important, I began making friends, something that, until then, had proven difficult for me because I had spent so much time away from campus for treatment.

I still had moments when I felt down, but the overall trend was again one of optimism. As I got further and further away from my last treatment and closer to the one-year mark of remission, I began feeling confident again that I would be cured.

My work with the college paper enabled me to get a temporary job at the New York Times and garner an internship for the upcoming summer in the Washington bureau of *The Wall Street Journal.* Upon hearing the news about my internship, a friend summed it up perfectly: "Your life is really coming together."

TWO DAYS AFTER moving to New York to begin my job at The Times, in December 1989, I called Dr. Shapiro to reschedule an appointment. He had taken over my treatment from Dr. Weeks in the summer of 1988. Before I could say anything, Dr. Shapiro cut me off, the urgency clear in his voice. "Brian, I've been trying to reach you," he said. "Your alpha-fetoprotein is slightly elevated. It may be nothing, but I want to have you checked again."

Terrified, I returned to Boston for blood tests and CT scans. The results were inconclusive. Every two weeks I repeated the drill, hopping the shuttle to Boston for more tests. Each time, the tumor marker climbed higher, yet a seemingly endless battery of blood tests, X-rays and CT scans yielded no trace of disease. Was it tumor, or was it something else, something less serious? No one knew.

At work and with my friends, I tried to carry on as if everything were normal, but the tension kept me on the verge of tears almost constantly.

By late February, with the alpha-fetoprotein doubling each month, Dr. Shapiro and members of Dana-Farber's solid tumor bone marrow transplant team became convinced that I had relapsed. A bone marrow transplant would be my best hope. The very high doses of chemotherapy now necessary would destroy my bone marrow. For that reason a portion of the marrow would be withdrawn before the chemotherapy was administered, frozen and then reinfused after my body had rid itself of the toxic drugs. This process is known as an autologous transplant.

Once they made their decision, the pace quickened. Everyday was important, they said. The smaller the amount of disease, the better my chances would be. I immediately left New York and returned to my family in Boston. The next day, I met with members of the transplant team, which comprises doctors and staff members from Dana-Farber and the neighboring Beth Israel Hospital. The informed consent document, protocol number 86-014, details the risks and possible side-effects of autologous transplant: heart failure, lung damage, kidney damage, liver damage—it reads more like an autopsy report than a description of a life-saving procedure.

Most alarming, however, is the conspicuous absence of the word "cure" from the protocol's list of objectives. In its place are phrases like "evaluate the side-effects of this chemotherapy" and "determine how effective high dose combination chemotherapy is against your tumor."

As I pored over the form, I could not help but suspect that, whether I lived or I died, it would not matter to the doctors because the data would be valuable in either case. Overcome with anger and frustration at finding myself once again bracing for chemotherapy, I leveled this charge at Dr. Shapiro. I instantly regretted it. His pained expression and the silence that followed reflected the depth of the hurt I had just inflicted.

Of course, doctors want desperately for their patients to get better. They realize, however, that medical science is not that simple. Cures are not developed over night. Often it takes years of experimenting and refinement. Thousands of others before me put themselves in similar situations in the process of developing the treatments that allowed me to live this long. I know this, and I try to rationalize it, but I still have a hard time accepting that I might not be the one who directly benefits from my treatment.

THE ONLY SURGERY involved in a bone marrow transplant is the harvesting of the marrow, a relatively minor procedure accomplished under general anesthesia by inserting a series of small needles into a bone between the hip bone and the spine. The doctors withdraw tiny amount, until about a quart is collected. This is preceeded by two cycles of standard VIP chemotherapy to eliminate as much disease as possible. After the harvesting, the patient receives massive doses of VP-16, ifosfamide and carboplatin.

The marrow is reinfused several days later, through an IV line, much like a standard blood transfusion. Once in the blood stream, the marrow cells home in and, if all goes well, take root and within several weeks begin producing the blood cells the body needs to carry oxygen, clot the blood and fight infection.

Although safer than donor transplants, autologous transplants are not

without risk. Despite advances in transplant technology, between five and fifteen percent of autologous transplant patients die from complications. Some die from the side-effects of the high doses of the toxic drugs, while others succumb to infections acquired during the time it takes for the transplanted marrow to begin producing enough white cells to fight infection.

On May 29, 1990, with the final pre-transplant tests and bone marrow harvest complete, one of the solid tumor transplant beds opened up.

A feeling of déjà vu swept over me as I walked through the lobby of the hospital to be admitted for the transplant. It seemed like only yesterday that I had first entered Dana-Farber as a scared 19-year-old. In some ways, much had changed. Yet, here I was, still suffering from a disease that is ususally curable. And still terrified.

By the time I reached the 12 West nurses' station—the transplant unit—to be admitted to the isolation room that would be my home for the next four to six weeks, I was an emotional wreck.

As much as I had tried to prepare myself for that moment, I was overwhelmed by the finallity of consenting to a treatment that could kill as well as cure. I could barely function as a nurse led me through the admission procedures and closed the door to my room.

The chemotherapy began that night and continued for the next three days. This period is a blank in my memory. The anti-nausea drugs kept me in a medicated slumber for most of that time.

When I finally came out of my groggy state, I felt remarkably good. I experienced some nausea and discomfort, but it was not as severe as I had expected. I felt relieved that I had survived the intensive chemotherapy without serious complications. This had been one of the doctors' greatest concerns, because I was born with only one kidney, which could have been fatally damaged by the toxic drugs. That initial sense of relief disappeared in the days that followed as the side-effects emerged.

On the third day after the end of the chemotherapy, the doctors returned my marrow. In an experimental procedure designed to reduce the risk of infection, they also reinfused two units of peripheral blood stem cells they had collected. These cells, which rapidly turn into red and white blood cells, are meant to act as a stopgap until the marrow recovers.

The actual reinfusion of the marrow, because it is only a transfusion, is considered one of the simplest steps in the treatment. However, the preservative used in the marrow and stem cells carries a strong, garlicy smell and taste. Within seconds of the cells entering my body, a weird senstation began building

continued on the next page

Who Knows. . .

in the back of my throat, followed by waves of nausea and vomiting.

Although I had received more than my share of chemotherapy over the years and had grown accustomed to the unpleasant side-effects, nothing could have prepared me for the next week. Intense nausea and diarrhea took over.

From the moment I awoke until I drifted off to sleep at night, I counted the minutes until my next dose of anti-nausea medication. But even the most powerful drugs lost their effectiveness after only an hour or so.

My spirit plunged. When you feel so sick, you cannot help wonder if you will ever feel better again. I was over-whelmed with despair. Autologous transplant patients usually recover their blood count and feel well enough to be discharged anywhere from three weeks to several months after receiving their marrow. I didn't believe I could hold out for the rest of the day, let alone three weeks.

This period was particularly difficult for my parents. My father's company had recently moved from Massachusetts to Georgia, and because his insurance was paying for my medical care, he stayed on with the company, flying back to Boston on weekends. This left my mother and sister alone in Boston and my father stuck hundreds of miles away, wishing he could be there to comfort me.

As I entered my second week, the nausea subsided and the blood count watch began. For days, my white blood count hovered near zero, leaving me dangerously susceptible to infection. Everything coming into my room had to be cleaned with a germicide solution, and all those entering had to wash their hands and wear gloves. Even my food had to be specially cooked to kill bacteria, then sealed in plastic.

Despite these precautions, I devel-oped a fever, as virtually all patients do. My infection responded to a regimen of antibiotics, and the fever broke almost immediately.

Several days later, however, a blood culture indicated that I had developed another infection. The team's of infectious disease specialist feared it was a candida, a potentially serious infection that could cause blindness or damage my heart valves. It was just such an infection that had killed my fellow patient Ron. The doctors initiated a more intensive antibiotic treatment using amphotericin, a drug that many patients refer to as "ampho-terrible" or "shake and bake" for the tremors and chills it often causes.

By the middle of that week, my blood counts began edging slowly upward. Then, 12 days after I had received my marrow, my white count skyrocketed, carrying my spirits with it. The danger from my fungal infection was now reduced, because my body had enough white blood cells to combat infection on its own.

My white count reached the safe level almost a full week sooner than expected, allowing the isolation to be terminated. One of my doctors, Karen Antman, flanked by two cheering nurses, did the honors, throwing open the door with a flourish.

Two days later, I was discharged and began my recovery at home. Originally, my doctors warned that I would proba-bly be laid up for three to six months. Five weeks after my release, though, I was working out and shooting baskets at the local park. At 10 weeks, I was back at work at The Times.

THE FURTHER AWAY from the transplant I got, the healthier I looked and the stronger I felt. My progress made my friends and my family ecstatic. Yet, for the first few months, I was more subdued. After having my hopes raised and then dashed so many times before, I had become wary of unbridled opti-mism. Moreover, I was painfully aware of the present limits of autologous transplants for testicular cancer. Al-though I knew transplants would cure some people, I could not help but recall the words of one of the doctors: "We get good responses, they just usually don't last very long."

But by late fall, with the X-rays, CT scans and tumor markers all normal, even I began thinking that, poor statis-tics or not, maybe I had finally beaten it.

That feeling was short-lived. At my routine November exam, Dr. Shapiro informed me that my alphafetoprotein was rising again. I slumped back against the exam table and rolled my eyes towards the ceiling; I could feel the tears welling up. It took all the courage I could muster to look at him and ask the question that I had always dreaded.

"Is this it?"

There was silence for a moment as Dr. Shapiro leaned back in his chair and sighed. "I have patients with tumors the size of golf balls all over their bodies," he began. "If they asked me if they were dying, I would have to say yes. But you're not dead, not by a long shot. You don't have bulk disease; it's not there. All you have is an elevated marker. Other than that, you appear perfectly healthy."

If I were to relapse, he continued, and the disease were limited to one localized area, it could possibly be surgically removed or treated with radiation. Or maybe it was not even a tumor causing the elevated marker; although unlikely, it was still a possibility, he said.

"Even if it does turn out to be disease, you might be able to live indefinitely with it," Dr. Shapiro said. "Who knows? You could outlive your doctor."

Dr. Shapiro may be right. I have already lived longer than many men at this stage of the disease. Every time I have approached the outer limit of medical science, something has come along to push that boundary further back. First it was the VIP regimen, then autologous transplants. Maybe someday refinements to the transplant process, like stem cells and growth hormones, will allow transplants to become the cure for which I and thousands of other testicular, ovarian and breast cancer patients are searching. △

Letters & Poems

Not Bill, Not Me!
Cheryl Morgan, MSW

As always I grew excited when I spotted my *Surviving!* stuck in my mail box. Each edition is packed with feelings, living, caring, and sadly this month, death.

I pulled the newsletter from my mailbox and immediately began scanning the pages while walking towards my office. Then I saw it; the picture of Bill Soiffer, his wife, and the article entitled "In Memory of Bill." I paused, feeling as if all the air had been sucked out of my lungs. Leaning against the wall to steady myself, I took a deep breath to stop the tears that had already begun to swell up inside of me.

How could this be? Not Bill, he's like me. . . . a comrade. . . a survivor. His writings brought strength to me, his will to live gave me energy when I needed it most . . . Not Bill!! And then, there it was the reality of this entire journey through diagnosis, treatment, and remission . . . a reality that often includes death. Why, how? Not Bill, not me, not Bill, not me . . . , strange, I'm having a difficult time keeping myself and Bill separated, but then . . . that's the point isn't it?

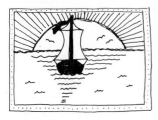

Two Poems by Melinda Lorenson

Last year, my grandmother died of a cancer that had started in her colon. I have a piece that I wrote at that time and one that I wrote recently. I hope readers who have lost friends or relatives to cancer will recognize that others have experienced such a loss. I also hope that readers with cancer will see that their cancer can cause relatives to learn just a little bit more about their relationships, and a lot more about their lives from your example.

Granddad is here
Not
grandmother and granddad
not Ruth and Al
just
granddad

When dad said
she's gone
I was fine:
Cancer
we were all
prepared.

Michele called
suddenly
preparation pointless
I cried:
she was
gone.

Tuesday night
picking out cello pieces
Playing each song through
judging
what was pleasant enough to play
at a funeral.

The family gathered for the funeral.

My cousin's young eyes
vibrant
But her tears only
streamed sorrow for
her grandmother's
death.

I was shunted to a balcony
transcending
the church
me and my cello
to remember
my grandmother.

For today
and tomorrow too,
I have more than
mere
memories
of my grandmother.

I remember our
sunny
healthy
days on our sailboat
before
cancer.

But
I learn from
frigid
emotional
hospital days:
she was the one who smiled

While the cancer
controlled
and stole
her body
her soul will always be
her own.

She did not really leave.

Her sturdy sailboat
sailed
beyond
our horizon:
Indeed
she still watches over me.

Now
I sail
onward
forward
toward
my own horizon.

111

I heard myself playing
"Happy recollections"
I only saw
my music and
my grandmother's
coffin.

I felt guilt
she was peaceful
patient
forgiving
generous:
everything I am not.
become.

She had the gift
serenity.
She must have
forgotten
to leave that gift
behind
for me.

Yet,
the horizon
wants me
to live
to learn
to stay in sight.

I feel challenged:
she was peaceful
patient
forgiving
generous:
everything I will try to

She obviously remembered
to show me
my sailboat
my wind
my hope:
I too can sail towards
serenity.

Poem by the William Callas family

Cancer knocked at our door.
Our lives changed forever more
Friends and Relatives will
              soon be no more. . .
Why? Can't they see! We
              are still the same!
Cancer is the one to blame
Is this a rare blessing,or
              a shame?
Cancer is to blame. . .
We stood by all, through their
              trials and ills
Knowing it's Cancer that kills
Few have chosen to see the light
As other live in a world
with no insight
Are all on earth so shallow
to see. . . Cancer, a disease
that came knocking at our door.
Forever life would not be
              the same. . .

Open your heart,
your mind and soul. . .
So you too may see who
could be at your
door!

My Life, Ambitions, and Goals
by Andria Callas

My goal is to graduate from Santa Rosa Junior College, with a degree in Applied Graphics, then transfer to Sonoma State University, for completion of my chosen vocation. My long-term goal is to work in an established art or architectural company. Upon graduating from Healdsburg High School, class of 1991, I ranked 28th in a class of 239, with a U.C. grade point average of 3.6 and a cummulative HHS GPA of 3.387.

I am an only child, and both my parents are senior citizens, living with several medical adversities. Since living the "roller coaster" ride of my father's metastatic prostate cancer, stage D1 diagnosis, I believe that with the many excellent opportunities available for education, people CAN face adversities in life. Thus, the importance of a college education, will not remain only in the classroom!

Currently, in my senior year of high school, I am spearheading the "New Horizons" club on campus. This is a support group for teens who are facing serious illnesses themselves, or who are involved with family or friends with health problems. The club is the first of its kind at Healdsburg High, and in fact, the Sonoma County area. I also intend to pursuit higher education, because all of our lives will have various adversities. . . whether medical, economical, religious, political, or vocational, we still can use our knowledge, as a necessity for LIFE'S SURVIVAL!

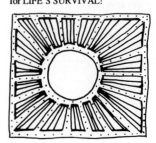

Surviving! is sincerely dedicated to Dr. Henry S. Kaplan, the former chairman of the Department of Radiology, at Stanford University Medical School. For many of us, his work has made "surviving" a reality.

Surviving! is a newsletter written and created by cancer patients, for the benefit of cancer patients and their friends and families. Our goal is to share common experiences and to help recovering patients manage the challenges of their illness, treatment and life after cancer. The Editorial Board welcomes letters from our readers about common concerns and issues present in the newsletter. We also welcome poetry, artwork or any information you would like to share which would be of interest to our audience.

Surviving! is made possible by grants from the Department of Radiation Oncology Stanford University Medical Center, and Varian Associates, Palo Alto.

 © **1992** , Stanford University Hospital

Fellow Survivors...Let us hear from you!
Write to us c/o Pat Fobair, at this address—

BULK RATE
U.S. POSTAGE
PAID
Permit No. 229
Los Altos, CA

Surviving!

c/o Stanford University Hospital
Department of Radiation Oncology
Division of Radiation Therapy, Room A035
300 Pasteur Drive
Stanford, California 94305

Address Correction Requested

THE COMMUNITY SERVICE WRITING PROJECT

Collaborative Introduction

Isela, David, Rosa, and Melinda wrote a collaborative introduction to the report. We have included the introduction and one page from the report that the students produced.

Collaborative Introduction to Ranking
of Newsletter Articles

Those involved with "Surviving!" are interested in compiling articles for a book dedicated to those affected by cancer. The purpose of the book is to provide an additional source of hope and encouragement for cancer patients and their friends and families. Topics include the complex issues of discovery, treatment, and recovery.

Since creating a book is an immense undertaking, the staff of "Surviving!" was looking for input from those not directly associated with the newsletter. As first-year students we have had the opportunity to work with them as an integral part of our English program. We have all been personally touched by cancer through our experiences with family members and friends. Working with the Patient Resource Center at Stanford Hospital, we were asked to read and respond to the articles in "Surviving!" Patricia Fobair was interested in our point of view as younger readers. Not only could we provide a different perspective due to our age, but we could also offer a fresh and unbiased view of the articles. We could provide an objective view because we are not acquainted with the writers of the stories.

To be honest, we first approached this project as an assignment; however, it soon evolved into an emotional learning experience. Each of us was affected by different aspects of the newsletters; some of us related to your stories, while others were deeply touched by your poetry. Nonetheless, our point is that you were all able to reach us in some way. You made a difference!

Thematic Analysis and Ranking of Newsletter Articles

The chart on pages 116–117 is taken from the students' thematic analysis and ranking of the three years of Surviving! *newsletter articles. The students read over 100 articles before making their choices. The "X"s on the graph indicate stories or articles that the students liked best.*

The main objective of our first meetings with Pat Fobair was to obtain information on the goals and organization for the upcoming book, since we wanted to base our editing method on a clear understanding of those goals. She said that the book would be divided into the four main areas of concern for cancer patients and their families: discovery, treatment, recovery, progression. Therefore, we based our editing method not only on choosing which articles were most moving, but also on the basic message of each article so that it could be properly categorized in the book.

We each had three years worth of articles to read, so we decided that going through each article as a group would not be reasonable. Instead, we decided that we would take three weeks away from the group meetings in order to read the articles on our own. Still, we needed to have a similar basis for discussion once we reconvened. So we each agreed to make a chronological chart of each article. We put an "x" in the column corresponding to the category that the article fit into, and only gave "x"s to the articles we liked best.

Once we met again as a group, we compared our individual charts. If we found inconsistencies in the choices of articles or in the categorization of those articles, we discussed those concerns. In our editing experience, we tended to find that either everyone liked an article, or, in the ones we did not like, other articles more aptly stated the information. In this way, we tended to choose the articles that were either the most personal, or the most thorough in describing their specific cancer experience. From all of that analysis and information, we were able to create the compiled chart seen on the following page. In accounting for individual and group ideas about any specific article, we were able to discuss, then, the merits of an article with Pat Fobair in an organized and professional way.

Date	Article	Discovery	Treatment	Recovery	Progression
Spt/Oct 89	"Courageous Cancer Recovery"	x			
	"Eye of an Illness"	x			
Nov/Dec 89	"Living Life"			x	
	"Rediscovering Yourself"			x	
	"Tragedy and Triumph"			x	
	"My Smaller Garden"				
	"The Art of Healing"			x	
Jan/Feb 90	"The Treasure of Life's Trauma"	x			
	"Each Day Is a Gift"	x			
Mr/Ap 90	"Glow Worm"			x	
	"The Hispanic Perspective"			x	
	"I Am Alive Afterall"			x	
	"Imagining"			x	
	"After the Losses"			x	
	"New Horizons"			x	
Jly/Aug 90	"I Didn't Give Myself Cancer"				x
	"Life After Work"			x	
	"Healing: Is It an Inside Job?"		x		
	"The Healing of a Wounded Warrior"		x		
	"Hodgkin's Is Here"	x			
	"The Ring of Life"				
No Date	"Surviving"	x			
	"Louise Renne's Quiet Fight"		x		
	"Gift From Denise"				x
	"Peace"			x	
Jan/Feb 91	"Trials and Tribulations"				x
	"The Winding Road of Beating Cancer"			x	
	"External Memories"	x			
	"Crab Walk"				
Mr/Ap 91	"A Woman's Choice"		x		
	"Moments of Ease"	x			
	"Massage"		Relationships		

My/Jne 91	"A New World" "Radiation Imagery" "I Remember" "One More Time" "In the Hospital" "Genes Are Your Destiny"		x x x x New Technology	x	
Jly/Aug 91	"Cancer: A Family Affair" "Feeling Lucky" "Sounds of Silence" "It's Strange" "Guardian"	x	Relationships	x x x	
Nov/Dec 91	"Life In the Shadow" "What Breast Cancer Taught Me" "Why I Chose My Family Over My Career" "When Bravery Is Irrelevant" "Little Ole Me"	x		x x x	

Thematic Analysis and Ranking of Newletter Articles

STUDENTS' EVALUATIONS OF THE PATIENT RESOURCE CENTER PROJECT

The following student evaluations will help you to understand the learning process of several of the students involved in the project. Since this casebook begins with Isela's journal, we conclude with Melinda's, Rosa's, and David's evaluations. Reading them will help you to better understand each of the student's complex learning experiences. Melinda focused her evaluation on what she learned about writing for others and the benefits of working collaboratively. Rosa's evaluation shows how her values and emotions were affected by the subject matter that she was thinking and writing about. David's evaluation is more reflective; his experiences at the Patient Resource Center helped him to put his own anxieties in perspective and to face the fear of loss and death that was tightly woven into the fabric of his life because of his father's leukemia and his roommate's struggle against Hodgkin's disease.

By Melinda Lorensen:

Community Service Writing: Collaborative Writing and Audience

In high school, I never had to write for a community service organization. In fact, the only audiences that I ever had to write for were my teachers, my peers, and myself. The community service writing project, therefore, was an entirely new experience for me. I thought the experience would seem difficult only because I would have to adjust my writing style for a new audience. Though I found this concern to be true, the greater triumph of the experience had less to do with writing and more to do with relating to others.

The little experience that I had had in high school with collaborative projects had been when teachers assigned the students with the highest grades to students who were struggling with a particular topic. I hated that idea because I always seemed to end up with the people who were not doing well, not because they were unable, but rather because they did not care about the subject. They were unmotivated. I came to hate group work because, in order for the assigned task to be completed, I always ended up doing all of the work.

In Freshman English my experience was a welcome change. Though one member of the group joined late, most of the work was evenly shared among the other three. I try to think back to what I will remember most from this project and I find that, though writing for a public audience was new, what I gained from the experience was a perspective of how to work in groups.

I called Pat Fobair to organize the first meeting, then I called David and Isela. We had to find a way to communicate effectively: we could not afford to have miscommunication lead to one of us missing a meeting. The stakes are higher when writing for a public organization: if I turn in a paper late, I only have to deal with the consequence of one teacher and one failing grade; if I miss a meeting with an organization, or, worse, a company, I am either out of a job, or I have the rest of the group feeling I am irresponsible. Dependability is essential with group projects. I now have a feeling for the importance of responsibility since three of us almost wasted an opportunity to meet with Ms. Fobair when she was half an hour late for a meeting at the Patient Resource Center. Without all the members of the group present, a collaborative effort collapses.

Our collaborative piece for *Surviving!* was made easier just by the fact that all four of us were responsible enough to make meeting times in order to write the piece. Flexibility is also necessary because with four people trying to meet, there are going to be times when you will need to bend a little, sacrifice a little, and make the meeting on time.

Since responsibility and flexibility were not problems with the group's collaborative piece for *Surviving!* we were able to focus on the writing itself. Because the article had to be brief in order to fit into the column in the newsletter, discussions over what the appropriate length would be for the given audience of 2000 subscribers were not necessary. Given the space constraint, we needed to focus on word choice. We often asked ourselves: How can we not only effectively convey our message, but efficiently convey that message for the given length? I found that collaborative writing was like having a super-thesaurus handy all of the time. I gained different perspectives of what words David, Isela, and Rosa thought were appropriate for a newsletter like *Surviving!* We would pick and choose from everyone's ideas about the best words to use for this particular audience, and I think the wording came out much better than it could have had any of us tried to write about the experience on our own.

Since there were four of us to deal with the question of audience, it was not like dealing with audience on my own, as I did with my poems about my grandmother. About halfway through the first draft of my second poem, I realized that I was no longer saying what I felt about the loss of my grandmother. I was writing about what I thought the audience would want to hear. How did I solve this problem? I took out my journal and began freewriting about my grandmother. What could I remember about her? Since she died a year ago, I asked myself how my attitudes about her life and illness had changed. I wrote quickly and I forgot my audience. Though forgetting audience may seem like a problem, my intention of writing in the journal was to do exactly that: I wanted to forget the audience for a while, and just remember myself. I lost my audience, but I found my grandmother in me.

The fact is, however, that I was writing for a magazine: in the final piece, I had to remember my audience. The audience of *Surviving!* is a sensitive one to write for since they read the newsletter for support in their fight against cancer. I did not want my piece to be depressing, though I still wanted to remain honest about my sad feelings about my grandmother. I wanted to be uplifting, but I did not want to appear unaware of the traumas of cancer, or ignorant about feelings of pain about the disease. The balance between me and my audience was a delicate one. I found that a merging of my original draft and my journal writing was an effective mixture of my voice and my audience's ear. Now it is up to the audience of *Surviving!* to decide whether my personal story helped them, and whether our collaborative piece was effective!

Though the audience does have ultimate control over the efficacy of our submissions to *Surviving!* we as writers can also reward ourselves. Four students and a contact person effectively functioned as a unit to create a product. Though working in a group was a challenge, one requiring responsibility and flexibility, when I finished writing for *Surviving!* I felt as though I had made a difference. Writing truly was its own reward. The best part about community service writing is that feeling of accomplishment: I did not just write my poem for myself and for a grade, I wrote my piece for an editorial board and for 2000 listeners. We let cancer patients and their families know that there are four students at Stanford that care very much about them. We all reached out, and hopefully, we helped someone.

By Rosa Contreras:

CSW Project: Patient Resource Center

"It started raining again! Maybe I should go downstairs and wait for the rain to stop." I turned away from the ATM machine and was about to walk down the stairs when I bumped into my friend Martin. Martin is a senior here at Stanford, and I met him in the beginning of the year, in my Italian class. "Hi!" I happily greeted him. "Hi," he quietly answered back. I could sense that something was wrong. "So . . . how was your Christmas break?" I asked him. Martin turned away, then looked at me in a sad, distant manner before he answered: "Remember that I told you that my father had been diagnosed with cancer a few months ago? Well, he died over break."

I looked up at his face, my eyes blinking through the rain, and felt so overwhelmingly sad; God! I did not know what to say. How could I possibly imagine what he was feeling at having lost his father in such a tragic manner? What do you tell a person whose loved one dies of such a horribly painful and sad disease? "I'm sorry" is just not enough. There are friends of mine who, in the past, have either personally battled cancer or have done it indirectly through their loved ones. I have loved ones today who are struggling daily against cancer. I feel so frustrated, so helpless, because I cannot ease their pain. What can I, as a human being, do to alleviate someone's pain, at least in a small way?

Since I have been affected by cancer through my experiences with loved ones, I became interested in working with the Patient Resource Center at Stanford University. Working with Pat Fobair and the *Surviving!* cancer newsletter, along with three other students—Melinda, Isela, and Dave—has provided me with an experience unlike any I have had before.

In the beginning, while I was aware that we would be working with cancer in some form, I really did not know what would be expected from us (Melinda, Dave, Isela, and myself) and in what manner we would perform a service for the many cancer victims and their loved ones. We soon found out that the people involved in putting together the *Surviving!* newsletter want to put a book together. This book will contain the articles from the newsletters since April 1987. The purpose of the *Surviving!* staff, through this book, "is to provide an additional source of hope and encouragement for cancer patients and their friends and families."

Reading those articles really touched me. I felt that I could relate to almost all of them because the experiences that the cancer patients described in their stories and poems are situations that I have lived through with my friends and relatives. There was one article that especially affected me. This article is entitled, "Young Author Writes About Cansur," and it was written by a young boy. This little boy wrote about his illness and tried to give hope to other children who have cancer. His article reminded me of a friend of mine, Beth, who had cancer when she was six years old.

Just as I have identified with many of the articles that will be included in the book, so will many other people. The articles range from the experiences of children to those of adults. The writers speak of the pain that cancer has given them and also of the courage that they have found to overpower this disease and continue living.

Participating in the formation of this book was a different experience from that of writing a paper for class. Rather than just writing about one's own experiences, as I have done, through this project I was able to read and learn a lot about the experiences of others. Learning more about the disease and its effects on its victims and their friends and families helped me to better understand what my loved ones have gone through and are still enduring. Now that

I know more about the different aspects of cancer, I can better understand and hopefully provide more helpful support to my friends and family.

By David Hollander:

CSW Evaluation

Imagine a confab around a 1960s hippie flower-cloth covered table. The participants are laughing, crying, and sharing. The location is the basement of the Stanford Hospital. The topics of discussion vary from good wieners to last weekend's trip to Yosemite, and the apprehension before chemotherapy. These people have at least one basic similarity: they all fight daily to reclaim their lives from the frightful disease of cancer.

In my Freshman English class I was given the opportunity to partake in a support group at the Patient Resource Center at Stanford Hospital. Initially, my job was to help edit back issues to compile a book of *Surviving!* newsletters. I was not too enthused at this option. The newsletter is a publication written by cancer patients who want to offer support and share their experiences with the disease. However, after considering some other possibilities, Pat Fobair, the Patient Resource Center head, and I agreed that I could partake in a cancer patient support group.

I chose to work with the *Surviving!* newsletter for a number of reasons. I felt like this would be ideal for me as I have had numerous experiences with cancer in my family and friends. For example, my best friend's mother died of leukemia. A close friend of mine who is a smoker potentially has breast cancer. My aunt has a tumor in her spine and is undergoing chemotherapy. My mother has had a biopsy on her breast. Foremost in my deciding to work with the newsletter rests in the fact that my father died of chronic leukemia three-and-a-half years ago. After a six-year struggle with cancer, a brain tumor, and pneumonia, the fatal infection won the battle and took my father from me.

Participating in this dynamic group, I heard and learned many valuable messages. I sat and listened to poignant and painful stories from these cancer patients. One had to drop out of graduate school. Another was in a foreign country, with limited use of the language, confronting leukemia by herself. Yet another is forced to do battle for the second time with a recurring disease. Their stories caused me to reconsider some ideas and questions regarding my philosophy on life and humanity, religion, and justice in this world.

I am very interested in philosophy and humanity. I have seen many life experiences pass before me. I cannot help but consider them in the "Big Picture" of life. I must place my feelings, thoughts, and self in perspective with all of the things around me. I run my brain in circles trying to answer my questions. I see that I am wary of smoking because my father smoked, contracted cancer, and died. However, I realize that I will die someday, beyond my control. But why expedite the process? Am I not afraid to die? Surely there are many things I have yet to accomplish and experience. Or, are these mere desires of the physical and all to be done in vain? It is this sort of thought process that haunts me. Often I spend nights tossing and turning, or arguing and sharing with similar thinking people.

So I continue to ask, "Why did these people get sick?" We briefly pursued this question during one of those Thursday afternoon sessions. Briefly, because the question is somewhat moot. These people aren't about negativity and pity. Hundreds of thousands of people contract cancer all the time. The ideal is not to harp on "Why are we sick?" but "Now that we're sick, what are we going to do? Sit around and die, or fight this disease with every gun we have?" I relate this wisdom to myself. I am angered at my selfishness and negative attitude. I have the flu and I complain about drowsiness, runny nose, and headaches. My problems are petty in comparison to those of these people who are holding on to last days and breaths. I am young, healthy, and strong. Does this make me a jerk? No, just a little ignorant, which happens to be my own pet peeve. It isn't surprising that I castigate myself.

I inquire one day: "Are you all (the group) religious? Do you find support in any one religion?" For the most part the answer is, "No. The world argues and fights over religion. We have our hands full in our fight with the disease inside our bodies!" I think to myself, How does this relate to me in my desire to understand and answer my questions? I wonder if it is futile for me to study philosophy and seek answers to the unanswerable. Perhaps I need to live every day and every minute to the fullest. But how?

The patients say that they have a new set of priorities after dealing with a life-threatening disease like cancer. "Oh yeah, I see now that the late-night hours to finish a paper, the small argument with my friend, the lack of money, it is all trivial. I'll sleep tomorrow and the paper will be turned in. My friend and I will still be friends. Money comes and goes. No sense in worrying about things I can't control." I realize that I have learned this through my father's death, through chronically ill patients, and through speaking with elderly people. I am somewhat calm, mellow, and sedated. I try to differentiate between transient factors and more permanent things in my life. Am I too pensive and tending toward indifference or laziness? Sometimes, it helps protect my sensitive inner self. This is a fine line that I must constantly reevaluate. There is no end. I question and reconsider different views at different stages in my life. It is my everlasting hope, yet ongoing battle with wisdom over ignorance.

Where am I after sharing with this group of special individuals? I have seen new lights and perspectives of people who are wiser than I. In a positive light, I want to help, perhaps dedicate my life to giving to people who are in dire need. Negatively, I wonder when it will be my turn. My risks of contracting cancer triple as it is prevalent in my heredity.

I refuse to let my selfishness take the better part of me. I cannot sit and watch and think as people suffer, fight, and die. At this moment, I await news from a biopsy performed on my roommate yesterday. Chances are high that he has Hodgkin's disease. No matter the outcome, I will support my friend. It is not only his struggle, but mine because I make it so. We are all bound by brotherhood. I want to help my brothers.

AGENCY'S EVALUATION: By Pat Fobair, Director

Name of Organization: *"Surviving" Newsletter*

Contact Person: *Pat Fobair* Phone Number: *(415) 854-5662, 723-7881*

Is the student's document effective? What are its strengths and weaknesses?

> *Review of newsletter stories over past 3 years—rated stories for content, chose best selections for possible book. Created a 2-page document which will help us in putting a book together. Their viewpoints reflected gender & age differences.*

In what ways will the student's work be of value to your organization? (Will the student's project be printed? How and to whom will it be distributed?)

> *We hope to create a handbook of patients' writings for new patients. They helped create an index of stories to draw upon for the editors of the new book.*

Please describe the nature of your interaction with the student. (How often did you confer with him/her? When given a specific responsibility, did he/she follow through conscientiously? Did the student turn in his/her paper on time?)

> *They met with me Jan 10, Jan 17, 31st, Feb 21, and March 6th. They followed through on all commitments on time. They collaborated well with each other in creating the index, calling each other and putting together the purpose statement & project summary.*

How did you help the student to complete his/her project (e.g., general orientation, helping him/her find resources and define topic, setting deadlines)?

> *I provided materials—2 newsletters from past years; by making regular times available (Fridays—1:30 pm)*
> *This was one of the more demanding projects in that they had to read and code 20 issues of the newsletter.*

Anything you'd do differently next time (e.g., start project earlier, provide more information and supervisions, instructor/agency writing goals)?

Things went well. We weren't sure how it would go—would it be too big or too small a task? It turned out I got what I wanted and they completed the task within the time frame.

Do you have any suggestions from improving the Community Service Writing Project?

Great idea! Unique experience for students, unique experience for me.

Melinda Lorensen
David Hollender
Rosa Contreras
Isela Franco

April 14, 1992

Dear Professor:

I am writing to compliment you on your innovative project ideas for Freshman English students. It was exciting for me to participate with four students on a common project. My need was to begin to organize the volumes of stories in the "Surviving" newsletter towards eventual publication in a different format. The students and I developed a mechanism. They chose the stories they liked best which would describe patients as they went through discovery, treatment, recovery, or recurrence. During the Winter quarter we met five times to review their progress and to maintain direction. They became more comfortable coming to the hospital and in talking about themselves. I was delighted with their choice of stories and enjoyed hearing how they felt touched by various experiences shared by the cancer patients in the newsletter. Conceptually it seems to me to be a very clever and useful idea to create projects for students to learn by helping others with a task that needs a boost to be accomplished.

The students' written work, a poem by Melinda and a group piece about what the project meant to them, will be published in the next issue of "Surviving" -- March/April. Enclosed is a copy of the student evaluation.

Thank you for offering. I benefitted from the delivery. There seem to be smiles all around. Maybe there is a role for next fall's students. Let's talk further.

                    Sincerely,

                    Pat Fobair, LCSW, MPH
                    Clinical Social Worker

INSTRUCTOR'S EVALUATION: By Marjorie Ford

In a teacher's final "accounting" and evaluation of an educational experience, be it in a writing, science, math, social science, or art class, the student's motivation is an essential concern. While motivation may develop in part from curiosity, an essential ingredient in the engagement with learning is ideally linked to caring—to caring enough to want to learn so that one can share what one has learned and help others. In this sense the community service writing model affirms the validity and value of service learning. Each of the students cared about their project; they were not learning simply for the reward of earning a grade. As Melinda concluded:

> Writing truly was its own reward. The best part about community service writing is that feeling of accomplishment: I did not just write my paper for myself and for a grade. I wrote my piece for an editorial board and for 2000 listeners. We let cancer patients and their families know that there are four students at Stanford who care very much about them. We all reached out, and hopefully, we helped someone.

At the same time, the project challenged the students intellectually. While reading, thinking about, and classifying more than 100 articles, the students were developing critical-thinking skills. Because they were being asked to read and make evaluations that would help to shape a professional publication for many readers, the students took their task seriously. They read carefully and thought deeply about what they read. On their own they had to develop criteria for analyzing, classifying, and evaluating a large number of articles. This task provided them with experiences that will be useful when they write research papers that involve selection, evaluation, and synthesis. In addition, simply being asked to make the selections was an excellent learning experience; it made them self-reliant and developed their self-confidence.

The students clearly succeeded. They worked together effectively, arranging all of their appointments with Pat Fobair and their own working meetings. Although it was a challenge for the students to write for such a large and sensitive audience, they overcame any misgivings they might have had. They gauged their audience accurately. Working with a minimal amount of supervision, charting new experiences off campus, they succeeded to a great extent because they were highly self-motivated and they cared.

From the very first day of class when Melinda, David, Isela, and Rosa told me that they wanted to have this opportunity to learn at the hospital because they had lost family members whom they loved, I was touched in a way that went beyond my professional role as their instructor. Because my own mother had died of cancer the year before, I was especially sensitive to their need to understand more about cancer. I found myself valuing Pat Forbair's wisdom and her capable handling of the students' intellectual questions and their feelings as well as her ability to guide all of us through their project.

Working with my students and attending *Surviving!* newsletter meetings made me aware of how other professionals function in the real world. More importantly, this experience made it clear to me that as teachers we are learners too. I still remember dreading the walk down the cold corridor to the oncology unit where Pat holds newsletter meetings. This walk will always connect me to the memory of the morning at the hospital after my mother's exploratory surgery when the oncologists told my sister and me that our mother had three months to live. I remember how my mother suffered during her last months; I will never forget how hard it was for all of us to say good-bye. Walking down that corridor to Pat's office, working with my students, I think we came a little closer to understanding how to face such losses.

CHAPTER 4

Sample Writing Projects

INTRODUCTION TO COMMUNITY SERVICE WRITING PROJECTS

Each community service writing project presents its own challenges and rewards. Although there is no way to predict the exact form that your project will take, it is possible to anticipate what may happen. Reading through the following models of student projects, followed by the student's or the group of students' evaluation, will give you valuable insights into what to expect from your experience working on a community service writing project.

The projects are divided into three sections. The first section features four projects in which each student's goal was to produce writing materials—such as newsletters, brochures, or fact sheets—for community organizations. Submitted to the instructor as a part of the students' course work, these projects were written to meet the needs of the agency. The writing project in the second section was submitted to the student's instructor. This essay integrates what the student learned while working at a community organization and through further research done to gain more insight into his or her service learning experiences. The third section includes students' reflections on their service learning experiences.

Section 1

The first three writing projects were included in newsletters. The writing completed for these projects is similar to the type of writing that you would do for an essay in a freshman or sophomore writing class or even for a humanities or social science course. Amy Gilliam's "Give of Yourself" was written for the *Ecumenical Hunger Program Newsletter*; the article describes her experiences working with and interviewing the women who were in charge of the shelter. Gilliam ends with a persuasive appeal to her audience. The second student project, a book review of *What Is a Wife Worth?* was written for the *Support Network for Battered Women Newsletter*. In the book review Amanda Hashfield employs a range of writing strategies—summary, analysis, research, and argumentation—as she clarifies how the point of view and the information provided by *What Is a Wife Worth?* helped her to better understand the complexities of a modern marriage.

The next project was written by a pair of students who had the challenge of designing a brochure to be included in a fund-raising letter for the Youth and Family Assistance program. The students working on this project were most concerned about persuading their audience "to appeal to their sense of civic pride and public responsibility." As the students gathered their facts and laid out the brochure, they knew they had the ammunition needed to show corporate leaders as well as average American families that they could "help real people with real problems."

Often a group of students will get involved in a longer project that requires considerable library research. Three first-year composition students working at the Peninsula Peace and Justice Center wrote and designed "The Central American Factpack," which profiles five Central American Countries. These students learned that the selection and presentation of facts can have political implications, deepened their understanding of current events, and came to better understand the importance of being concise as they struggled to present their extensive research in the compact two-page fact sheets.

Section 2

The next two papers developed out of the students' experiences volunteering at a community organization. After working with inmates at the Juvenile Detention Center over a period of two years, Euclid Zubaran in "Does the Juvenile Justice System Work?" discusses the reasons why so many of the youths return repeatedly to the Detention Center. Among other issues, Zubaran points to the dysfunctional family units that do not provide adolescents with positive activities to keep them off the streets and out of trouble; he argues that juvenile detention centers need the help of the community if they are to offer enough support to help juvenile delinquents to shape productive lives. The second research essay, "Service Learning: Education with a Purpose," was written by Jeremy Taylor, one of the students who worked on the Reach Out newsletter project that is included in Chapter 3. Taylor's project inspired him to find out more about the reasons why many educators today believe that service and academic learning should be linked.

Section 3

Service learning is far more than just the production of projects and papers. Perhaps what becomes most meaningful for many students is the personal growth that they experience as they reflect on their service learning experiences. In her community service journal, Jennifer Hancock reflects on her process of producing a series of environmental fact sheets for the Conservation Corps and a related research paper. It is exciting to see her growing awareness of the complexity involved in a research paper, of the importance of interpersonal relationships, and of the need to be patient and yet determined when faced with technical problems. Hancock's journal presents a concise and clear record of the ways in which a student's critical-thinking skills can develop through working on a service project.

The next two reflective essays say more about how students' values and attitudes about education have changed through their service experiences. After completing an informational service project on the California tiger salamander, Justin Augustine wrote "Reflections," in which he explores his changing perspective on the meaning of grades and the satisfaction of volunteerism:

> Write a paper, get a grade, write a paper, get a grade, write a paper, get a grade. . . . The Community Service Writing Project put an end to that monotonousness. It added a new dimension to my writing. People. Real people would be reading this article. . . . the satisfaction came from the fact that my writing was being used for a positive purpose, in this case, educating the public. And that's what volunteerism is about—performing a service for others and receiving satisfaction as pay.

The concluding selection by Lam Nguyen explores the lessons he learned about the value of life from his experiences volunteering at an AIDS hospice. In his essay "Room 653," the room comes to embody what Nguyen knows will happen, why he has faith, and how helping makes him feel that he can make a difference.

We think that you will find yourself engaged by the issues brought up in these projects. We encourage you to read the evaluations as well as the projects. Each of you will find different meanings in them, different lessons to learn about writing and about living.

SECTION 1: WRITING PROJECTS COMPLETED FOR SERVICE AGENCIES

Ecumenical Hunger Program

Ecumenical Hunger Program

Purpose

The Ecumenical Hunger Program provides emergency food, clothing, furniture, and other assistance to people experiencing emergency hardship in Palo Alto, East Palo Alto, and Menlo Park. Recognizing that hunger is but one of many problems low-income families face, EHP is committed both to responding to immediate need and to helping families address the root causes of their situation.

EHP provides an average of 1500 people every month with an emergency supply of groceries. While alleviating immediate need remains a major focus of EHP's work, EHP also assists families in moving toward greater independence and self-sufficiency by working with families to locate resources for jobs, housing, health care, and education and by acting as an advocate with other social service agencies.

Writing Tasks

* Write a ''Daily'' article on students volunteering at EHP.
* Write EHP public information fact sheets.
* Research hunger and poverty issues and write feature stories for the newsletter.

* Interview EHP staff, volunteers, and families and
  write personal profiles for the newsletter and
  "The Observer."
* Write a profile of families that have received
  assistance; this document will be sent to the
  Peninsula Community Foundation, which helps to
  fund EHP's work.

Give of Yourself

Amy Gilliam

"Good afternoon, EHP," I said. There was an uncomfortable pause, and then the female voice at the other end of the line began hesitantly in Spanish. My Spanish background being quite limited, I thought it only fair to warn her, "Yo hablo un poco Espanol. . . ." I could sense her relief upon hearing her native language as she began again, this time faster and more fluidly. I was completely lost. "Un momento por favor," I said desperately, frantically scanning the office for a potential translator.

This was my first afternoon to volunteer at the Ecumenical Hunger Program, and the Director, Nevida, had asked if I wouldn't mind answering the phone. No problem, I thought. I did not know what I was in for. One of my fellow volunteers, Lorraine, was packing food boxes in the back while Heather, who lived in my dorm, had been in the clothes closet distributing clothes to the needy families. Basically those who volunteer at the Ecumenical Hunger Program do whatever needs to be done on any particular day. We were all glad to help in any way we could but felt self-conscious about making mistakes, untrained as we were. In spite of these blunders, "the volunteers at EHP are indispensable," according to Lisa, the Food Coordinator.

In fact, Lisa herself, an energetic black woman in her early twenties, started out as a volunteer at EHP under the wing of her mother, the director. This service-oriented family began at the Red Cross, where Nevida worked and Lisa volunteered as a young girl. "I have always wanted to help people," Lisa explained. So when her mother moved on to EHP in 1978, Lisa went along. Yet Lisa was not hired by EHP as "the daughter of Nevida." Instead, in 1982, she was offered a job in her own right when her mother took a leave of absence.

The project has many goals and functions, including the provision of emergency food, clothing, and furniture to individuals and families in need, and the coordination of local resources to locate housing, jobs, educational opportunities, counseling, and health care for these people. Yet sometimes, Lisa explained, these "emergency" situations become recurring ones. "Some families come in here year after year," Lisa said. "In fact, I have been seeing one family for five years now." Due to the problem of illegal immigration, many large Hispanic families encounter economic problems at the end of each month. The cycle is a vicious one, Lisa told me, because these people are only able to obtain jobs that offer minimum wage and pay in cash. In addition, they must support the many children who are often found in Hispanic Catholic families. Lisa observed, "Oftentimes, a woman will come in with a new baby each year."

Thus, some families become more or less dependent upon the help of EHP at the end of the month due to circumstances that are out of their control. In extreme cases, EHP will provide cash to supplement rent payments, but the staff at EHP tries to veer away from this practice and stick to more "therapeutic" measures. They explore all avenues for reducing this dependency, such as, for example, their job referral service. EHP remains in close contact with many local businesses that keep the program in touch with their job opportunities. Also, the EHP staff has often attempted to bring large families together in cooperation. This method allows for one parent to assume responsibility for child care while the others seek employment. The extra wage earner can often help tide the families over.

Unfortunately, not all of these clients have quite as valid reasons for their need. That is why keeping records on them is so important at EHP. Lisa explained the necessity of the formal request for food supplement. She pointed out that it does not probe into the personal life of the applicant but simply asks for statistics such as income and family size. Lisa's concern was that the program not be thought of as "a free handout." The only time EHP confronts problems of this sort is when drugs are involved. Because the local community harbors a frighteningly large population of drug users, the staff at EHP takes measures of caution to be certain that their emergency help with food and clothing is not taken advantage of. This happens when the individual receiving aid uses any money available for drug purchases while depending on the program for necessities. That is why records are kept on the clients, applications are required, and interviews are utilized. If drug addiction is suspected, Lisa explained, the staff will not turn the individual away but instead will take the person into the EHP kitchen and make him or her a meal. This practice satisfies the person's immediate need yet does not allow the individual to become dependent on the organization as a source of food.

I could tell that the drug problem truly disturbed Lisa because of its effects on the children of the community. Her concern for these children was made quite evident throughout the interview as she described how not only some go hungry even after receiving help (because of their parents' addiction), but also how they are raised in an atmosphere that perpetuates the same problems over and over. "I have been here long enough to see the children of clients become clients themselves," Lisa observed sadly. The way EHP tries to remedy this situation is to concentrate on these underprivileged children. In the future, the staff is planning an after-school program where the children can participate in planned activities and be provided with food. "What they really need is for someone to care for them and love them. It has probably been a long time since they heard the words 'I love you.'" One could tell from the look on

Lisa's face that she wished she could do this for each and every one of them. It saddened me to hear Lisa's story about the teachers who would call from school to complain that some of the children in their classes were hungry. "By the way the children tore into their food at lunch, the teachers believed that the kids hadn't eaten since the day before," Lisa said.

Upon hearing this, one wonders, "what can I do to help these children and their families?" Of course, food, clothing, and furniture donations are always appreciated at EHP. Yet, hands-on assistance has a more lasting effect. Volunteers help out with the work, but more importantly, they contribute a little of themselves to the program. A volunteer working in the clothing closet has those extra few minutes to pay attention to the child whose mother is juggling her other children while sorting through the clothes. Thus, when considering what one can do to help, one should remember that the gift of time can be the most precious one.

PROJECT EVALUATION: By Amy Gilliam

1. I decided to work on the Ecumenical Hunger Program for my real writing project because I had volunteered there in the fall and the staff there had struck me as being dedicated and sincere. Therefore, I called the director (a number of times because they are extremely busy there) and was eventually set up with an interview with her daughter, Lisa. The interview proved to be very helpful and gave me quite a bit of information about the program. I was considering also interviewing a client-family but ran into so many problems trying to set it up with the staff at EHP that I changed my mind and decided to draw upon my own experiences as a volunteer at EHP. My assignment was to write an article for the newsletter.

2. I found this project quite interesting because I was faced with the prospect of writing for an audience I had never considered writing for before. As opposed to writing for a teacher, instructor, or student peers in an "academic" setting, I was communicating to the public on a different level. I found myself using less complicated vocabulary and sentence structure and (upon suggestion) attempting to be more concise than I am accustomed to.

3. As I mentioned above, I had quite a bit of trouble contacting the public service organization and its staff. They are extremely busy there so I completely understand their level of disorganization, yet I would not suggest depending on them for a real writing project. Often I had trouble catching my contact person at the office.

Support Network for Battered Women

Support Network for Battered Women
Mountain View, CA

Purpose

The Support Network for Battered Women provides
services to battered women and their children and to
all other members of the abusive family. Services
include a 24-hour crisis line, support groups, peer
counseling, clinical counseling, legal aid, a
residential shelter, child care, group work,
information and referrals, and community education.

Five times a year, the Support Network produces a
newsletter (circulation 6,000) which contains
articles on the extent and nature of domestic
violence, its causes and social costs, and potential
solutions.

Writing Tasks

* Write a review (approximately 500 words) for the
  newsletter describing a book or movie dealing with
  domestic violence.
* Write an article for the newsletter (e.g., violence
  and pop culture). Previous articles have discussed
  TV violence, the Support Network's Crisis Line, and
  a son's view of his mother's recovery. Other topics
  include: marital rape, changing police procedures
  in domestic violence calls, attitudes about domestic
  violence, shelters for battered women, laws
  regarding domestic violence, etc.
* Write feature articles for local newspapers on
  individuals in the organization making outstanding
  contributions and on Network events and programs.

> * Write handouts on various topics (e.g., A.A., peer
> counseling, self-help groups, self-esteem) for the
> volunteer training program. Rewrite handout on
> children of domestic violence.

What Is a Wife Worth?

Amanda Hashfield

You are female and standing with a group of women at a party. The subject of work comes up. "I'm a litigation attorney." "Oh, that must be exciting. I work with computers." "Really? My husband does that. I could never deal with all that math and science. I like to work with people; I'm a psychologist. And what do you do?" "Me, I'm just a housewife."

Unfortunately, this little scenario show how most people still think. A housewife's production is not included in the country's GNP. Neither Social Security nor the U.S. census recognizes her work. That's why matrimonial lawyer Michael H. Minton wrote his book, *What is a Wife Worth?*

So just what is a wife worth in a marriage? Courts figure out worth by looking at what each spouse economically contributes to the marriage. For the husband, it's usually his salary. Minton tried to figure out the same thing for the wife. He listed the roles that a wife fills, from food buyer and cook to chauffeur and secretary to interior decorator and child psychologist. His list includes twenty-four different tasks and how many hours each week a home-maker devotes to each task. After multiplying these by their hourly rates in the marketplace and by 52 for a yearly rate, Minton came up with a salary of over $40,000 a year as a wife's worth, or how much it would cost to hire someone to take a wife's place. The chart at the end of this article was created for a divorce case he was trying. The judge was so convinced by his reasoning that the client was awarded that sum as yearly maintenance for her contributions to the marriage.

Previously, courts had simply given property to the person whose name it was in, which was often the husband. Between 1970 and 1983, though, most states adopted some form of the Uniform Marriage and Divorce Act, whereby division of property is based on the contribution of each partner to the mar-riage . . . and homemaking counts as an equal contribution. This is best sum-marized in the *University of Florida Law Review* (vol. XXVI, p. 221):

> Absent the services rendered by the homemaker wife, the husband would be
> forced to seek such services elsewhere at personal expense. By performing
> daily domestic chores, the housewife frees the husband to concentrate his
> efforts entirely on the business. Hence the homemaker should be entitled to a

partnership share in the same manner as the wife who participates actively in the family business.

With this law, many states recognized that both the husband and the wife contribute *equally* to the marriage; the husband's part is just more visible.

But wait a minute! Don't husbands help around the house, too? Especially if the wife works outside the home? Apparently not. Minton found that a full-time homemaker spends an average of 99.6 hours a week on household work. Her husband will help for an hour and a quarter. But that's fair, right? House-work is all she has to do and he's tired from a long day at the office. So what happens when the wife is also coming home from a rough day at the office? The studies Minton looked at found that when the wife works outside the home, the amount of housework done by the husband doesn't go up. It doesn't even stay the same, but drops to 36 minutes a day.

Minton provides a thorough and convincing argument on a wife's worth. In a critique of the book, though, Jean Windle Friedricks (*Best Sellers*, Vol. 43, February 1984, p. 420) finds a few problems with Minton's too literal transla-tion of a homemaker's tasks to those performed in the marketplace. In the "real world" a professional's salary is determined by factors other than just the work done: there are degrees held, work experience, and how well the job is done. There's also the constant threat of being fired if the work is not good enough. Another problem with his calculations is that not all tasks are per-formed on a regular basis, 52 weeks a year. Minton doesn't take this into consideration since everything is blindly multiplied by 52. The last objection was that the book seems to pertain only to middle- and upper-middle-class women. That's the type Minton generally represents in divorce cases.

Minton talks about a wife's worth only in terms of the tasks she does and the dollar value assigned to these tasks. This is not to say that this is all a wife contributes to a marriage. Both partners contribute much more. But they're intangibles like love and companionship. You can't place a dollar figure on them. The purpose of Minton's book was to determine the dollar value of a wife's work and that's why these less definable contributions were not in-cluded. This book was written by a divorce lawyer, but it's a book about mar-riage. Because it serves to tear away the image of "just a housewife," it should strengthen the concept of marriage as a partnership between two equals.

You can find *What Is a Wife Worth?* at the Support Network's library, or check with your local librarian.

PROJECT EVALUATION: By Amanda Hashfield

Write an essay. Ok, I have a week to do it; I'll worry about it later. Suddenly it is the night before the essay is due. I want to do well on it, but I also do not want to witness another sunrise. Oh well, so the teacher won't have that high an opinion of me. Maybe I'll get comments like, "Good ideas, but they don't seem to be completely worked out." So I get a bad grade; worse things have happened in life.

At some point in life almost everyone has left writing a paper until the last minute, and some of the above thoughts have probably run through that person's mind. The worst things that happen if that person hands in a shoddy paper is that the teacher is disappointed and the student receives a bad grade. The fear of these consequences is sometimes not enough to motivate a student to put a lot of effort into a paper which does not interest her. The entire scenario changes when the student is writing for a public service agency.

It is no longer just the teacher who is reading the paper; the essay is going to be published, and your name will be at the top of it. The writing matters. People care what you have to say, and that makes you care about what you are saying. You no longer feel that what you are writing is irrelevant, a topic created just so you can prove to the teacher that you really do know what a thesis is. With a real writing project, the topic exists and needs to be written about; if you do not write the piece, someone else's time will have to be spent working on it. The real writing assignment seems to give Freshman English more of a purpose than just learning how to write a comparative essay.

For my assignment, I wrote three articles for the Support Network for Battered Women. One article was a book review, one was on acquaintance rape, and one was an interview with a survivor of wife abuse. The article that had the most effect on me, personally, was the interview. What this woman went through was amazing. Somehow I wanted the article to have the same impact on the readers that the woman had on me. I did not want the readers to be able to distance themselves; I wanted them to feel the gun that was pointed at the woman and to know what incredible courage it took for her finally to walk away from her husband and her life. This article was also important because, not only was it going to be published and read by a lot of people, it was going to be read by the woman I interviewed. I was telling her life; the grade I received really did not matter. What mattered was telling her story the way she would want it told.

Everyone writes differently. My former roommate spends a half hour typing randomly onto her computer, then sees what she has written and starts organizing her paper. I agonize over each word on the first draft and then do very few revisions. I also do not keep a journal; I organize things in my head. If someone else collects her thoughts better by seeing them on paper, then a journal probably is a good idea. The journal should not be a requirement. If it is, then it just becomes another thing to be done for no other reason than to prove to the teacher you did it.

Writing for an agency takes more time than a standard 15-page research paper would. It also takes more effort, to get to the agency and to obtain the material needed, which generally is not found in a library, such as a human being for an interview. In the end, though, you do not notice that you are spending more time, because your time has a purpose, and you care.

Write an essay. For the first time in my life I started today and not the day before it was due.

Youth and Family Assistance

Youth and Family Assistance
Redwood City, CA

Purpose

Youth and Family Assistance works with at-risk young
people and adults on the San Francisco peninsula,
providing a continuum of prevention and intervention
services designed to resolve crises and divert
problems from the legal system. YFA coordinates
eight family assistance programs; examples include
Your House, which reunifies families separated as a
result of runaway youth, chronic communication
problems, or abuse; the Community Living Room, a safe
place for homeless youth to gather; the Redwood
Therapeutic Day School, which guarantees an
educational environment for youth who cannot be
served on a regular high school campus.

Writing Opportunities

* Develop a brochure to be inserted with fund-raising
  letters. The brochure should be short; ideally
  Stanford students working on this project will have
  skills in photography and layout as well as in
  writing.
* Produce a five-minute audiotape based on interviews
  with YFA clients.

Note: The YFA office has a great deal of detailed,
current information about problems faced by families
and at-risk youth. Student writers who produce
materials for YFA are welcome to make use of these
resources in writing research papers for class.

Brochure

YOUTH AND FAMILY ASSISTANCE
Working to help your community

Did you know . . .

- Fewer than 3 percent of all American families have two natural parents
- More than one-third of all California children never complete high school
- The Juvenile Hall in San Mateo County has enacted a cap on admissions due to overcrowding
- Over 1000 teenagers leave home each year in San Mateo County
- 30 percent of all girls and 15 percent of all boys in the U.S. are sexually abused by the age of 18
- Substance abuse is proven to have significant negative effects on families, friends, co-workers, and children of addicted individuals

YOU CAN HELP

Your donations can help Youth and Family Assistance stop the continuing cycles of juvenile crime, homelessness, substance abuse, and violence. With your help, we can clean up our community and stop the deterioration of youth. Our programs address these problems at the source, preventing their growth and saving the taxpayer from long-term economic burdens. Give us, the kids, and your community a helping hand!

Our Programs deal with . . .

AIDS Education
- Involves peers in an AIDS program
- Attempts to warn homeless youth of the high risk of AIDS involved with drugs and prostitution

Drug and Alcohol Abuse
- Works with local school districts and justice systems to prevent abuse by youth
- Educates first-offender drunk drivers and diverted drug offenders
- Provides individual counseling and group support services
- Supports youth with a substance intervention project
- Offers a drop-in referral center for at-risk youth

Family Violence
- Impacts violence in society through education regarding child abuse, abusive relationships, and elder abuse

- Raises public awareness through free presentations and community conferences
- Counsels abuse victims in crisis
- Sponsors personal workshops for parents and children
- Offers a therapeutic, non-legal setting to help spouse abusers end destructive patterns

Child Homelessness
- Offers non-institutional, safe settings for homeless youth in San Mateo County; provides food, housing, mental health education, employment needs, and medical care in a relaxed atmosphere
- Provides young people with individual living skills, building their self-sufficiency
- Coordinates closely with other government and community service agencies
- Offers unique, active involvement of volunteer mentors who serve as supportive role models
- Provides youths with a safe place to wait while family tensions subside

Education
- Reduces number of school dropouts by running a counseling program directly on school campuses
- Encourages achievement for street youth through education employment incentive programs
- Provides for the special educational needs of emotionally disturbed youth
- Offers small, less frustrating classroom settings, allowing for greater individual development

Juvenile Crime
- Prevents delinquency by working with the community to guarantee positive peer and parental support
- Works closely with local police to provide constructive alternatives for juvenile offenders
- Adolescent diversion program provides professional counseling for first-time juvenile offenders
- Programs decrease congestion in juvenile halls, local prisons, and probationary systems

Family Counseling
- Strengthens families through parent education programs
- Provides individual, group, and family counseling
- Provides long-term residential counseling for victims of abuse, sexual abuse, and neglect
- Places emphasis on professional family counseling, strong parental involvement, and eventual family reunification

Behavioral Counseling
- Assists youth in understanding the underlying causes of their actions and in controlling their behavior; provides assistance through individual emotional counseling
- Helps youth set and achieve social goals that are important to them
- Teaches youth to tear down negative self-images

Runaway Youth Assistance
- 24-hour response to family crisis situations
- Reunites runaway youth with their families or finds a safe and permanent alternative
- Saves runaways from an inevitable life on the streets

AUDIENCE ANALYSES FOR YOUTH AND FAMILY ASSISTANCE: By Chad Herrin and Kay Hong

Chad wrote his analysis after getting his placement at this organization but before he got the specific assignment:

The writing opportunities for this program will include brochures and fund-raising letters. I believe writing for this project will be directed toward two separate and different groups: the at-risk young people and adults in the area and the private sponsors that contribute funds to the program. The people in the sponsor group could range from corporate sponsors to average American families. The message I must send to these people must be quite different. I must appeal to their sense of civic pride and public responsibility. They must understand that they can help real people with real problems. Sponsors must get the impression that their contributions are desperately needed. After reading my brochures, the people in this audience must feel they have a worthy, important cause in which they can invest.

Our writing for the at-risk people will be much different than the tone in my writing directed toward the sponsors. The writing for the people that are assisted by the program must appeal to their sense of need. The articles must convince them that there are programs that will be beneficial to them and their children. My articles must also appeal to young homeless or runaway youth. It is important that the writing is clear enough for children, but it is also important that the writing is comfortable and believable. The tone of the writing is also critical, and I must make sure that the articles don't sound condescending. The audience that reads my writing must get the impression that there is a safe and helpful place that they can go to for help.

Kay wrote her analysis after their peer group got their specific writing assignment for YFA:

The Youth and Family Assistance organization works to avoid the legal system in dealing with social issues that may be handled poorly if forced through the courts. Dealing with at-risk youngsters and adults, the YFA coordinates several programs to lend aid specifically to family assistance.

The CSW project we are doing for YFA asks specifically for a brochure to be inserted with fund-raising letters. Instead of readers who need to be persuaded to take advantage of the YFA, the target audience will most likely consist of corporation heads or the chairs of their philanthropy departments, governmental organizations, and everyday people ranging from the working class to the economically elite. The inclusion of working class and the lower-middle class as potential donors is due to the empathy factor. Time and time again, a large portion of donations come from those who give though they can't afford it. If they can't donate their money, they may often donate their time. As many working-class or lower-middle-class adults may be single-parent heads of households, many may have, at one time or another, needed to take advantage of the services offered by YFA and will understand the plight of those who do. The main goal of this brochure should be to target the "empathy factor" even in terms of the financially well-off. If the entire audience can be made to empathize rather than sympathize, more donations in terms of both money and time should come through.

Peninsula Peace and Justice Center

Peninsula Peace and Justice Center
Palo Alto, CA
Contact Person: Paul George, Coordinator

Purpose

The Peninsula Peace and Justice Center seeks to
bring together individuals and groups to work for
peace and social justice. Forty-four member groups
and approximately one thousand individuals belong
to the Center. The Center hosts a variety of community programs and events and provides information,
resources, and referrals through a speakers bureau,
video production team, Peace Resource Directory, and
hotline.

   The Center also publishes a monthly newspaper,
''Peace Works.'' Peace Center Coordinators have
worked with volunteers on the newspaper since the
Center's beginnings in 1982. Participation of
students and other volunteers has enhanced the
quality of the newspaper.

Writing Opportunities

* Write newspaper articles on selected peace and
  social justice issues.
* Attend and report on selected Bay Area events
  (e.g., Mideast vigil; nuclear disarmament meeting;
  ''Women as Peace Workers'' meeting).
* Interview Peace Center speakers and write articles
  for the newspaper (300 to 800 words).
* Write a newspaper profile (750 words) on each of
  the thirty-four member groups.
* Write press releases.

* Edit and shorten material for the monthly newspaper
  (e.g., condense three-page articles into one-
  paragraph "News for Activists" briefs).
* Research and write up reports on countries where
  the United States has a military presence. Full
  reports will be kept in the agency's files for
  internal use; one- to two-page fact sheets will be
  used to brief activists, possibly for distribution
  to high school classes, etc.

Central American Factpack

Lynn Deregowski

Greg Scown

Derrick Sung

EL SALVADOR

Statistics:

Population: 5,400,000 (1989)
Area: 8,260 square miles
Leader: Alfredo Cristiani Burkard
Principal language: Spanish
Principal religion: Roman Catholicism
GNP: $4.0 billion (1986)
Literacy rate: 72% (UNESCO)
Education: secondary enrollment 15%
Average income: $820 per capita
Debt: $2.2 billion (1987)

Background

During the 1500s, El Salvador was incorporated into the Spanish Empire by
Spanish conquistadors. These Spanish
conquerors massacred thousands of
native Indians, initiating the trend of
internal death and destruction which has
existed in El Salvador ever since.

By the late 1800s, coffee was the primary export and source of wealth for El
Salvador. The coffee created a small,
incredibly wealthy oligarchy, leaving the
rest of the population practically destitute. Not surprisingly, U.S. capitalists
sought their fortunes in the country, and
the U.S. became the principal foreign
influence in El Salvador by 1900.

Most of the Pipil Indians lost their
communal lands and were forced to
work on coffee plantations. However,
with the onset of the Great Depression,
coffee prices fell, and thousands of
Indians lost their jobs. Thus, in 1932, the
Pipil Indians rose in a rebellion which
was brutally put down as the Salvadoran military, under the leadership of
General Maximiliano Hernandez Martinez, slaughtered thousands upon thousands of Indians. The remaining Indians
abandoned their culture to prevent any
future massacres. General Martinez

remained the dictator of El Salvador until 1944.

As conditions for the rural population worsened, many of the poor landless peasants emigrated to Honduras. This caused tension between El Salvador and Honduras, who blamed the Salvadorans for many of Honduras' problems. The tensions escalated to a one-week war in July 1969. After the war, the landless peasants of El Salvador could no longer escape across the border. Thus, internal friction between the wealthy oligarchy and the destitute peasant workers increased. Mass movements of students, workers, and peasants against the dictatorship arose. By the mid-1970s, the Salvadoran government was using violence to control these mass organizations.

Military Opposition

Leftist guerilla organizations formed in El Salvador during the early 1970s. The strength of these organizations remained minimal until March 1980 when four separate guerilla organizations unified to form the Unified Revolutionary Directorate (DRU). In October 1980, the DRU renamed themselves the Farabundo Marti Liberation Front (FMLN). The FMLN waged guerilla war against the government but could not attain political power because the United States heavily supported the Salvadoran government. Thus, the FMLN resorted to a prolonged war of sabotage and mini-assaults to gradually weaken the government.

Military Response

The Salvadoran death squads began to arise in the mid-1970s. Throughout the country, these deadly forces sought to terrorize and eliminate the leaders of the mass peasant organizations. Finally, in 1984 the U.S. announced that military and economic aid would be cut off if the death squad violence did not cease. After this announcement, death squad violence did drop significantly.

Military Political Rule

In October 1979, a new junta government replaced General Carlos Humberto Romero. Although the junta promised reforms, it could not stop right-wing military violence. A second junta proved as ineffective as the first and lasted until March 1980 when Jose Napoleon Duarte of the Christian Democrats (PDC) became leader of the third junta. Although Duarte remained in power until March 1982, the military still held the real power in El Salvador.

Duarte regained power in the election of 1984, but only with over ten million dollars in U.S. aid. The elections were boycotted by the FMLN, and guerilla violence resulted in low turnout. The high military officers and important members of the private sector threw their support behind Duarte because they knew they could control him. Sure enough, under Duarte the wealthy oligarchy still controlled the economy, and the military was still the main source of power.

Duarte & Human Rights

On December 11, 1981, the Salvadoran army slaughtered 1200 peasants in a single day as part of its "scorched earth" policy to drive people out of eastern El Salvador in an effort to get at the FMLN. In one week in October 1983, over 200 civilian murders were reported. Duarte made mostly cosmetic changes in response to these atrocities. Under Duarte, the Salvadoran government opened negotiations with the FMLN. Negotiations with the FMLN broke down quickly, and Duarte's popularity began to slide dramatically.

Following a large electoral success in September 1984, the government launched extensive health, education, and government services reforms, which have yet to be implemented. Duarte's popularity was again wounded by his handling of the kidnapping of his daughter by guerrillas. His controversial austerity measures introduced in January 1986 incited strikes and protests, and relations with the Roman Catholic church became considerably colder.

Negotiations with the FMLN

President Duarte offered, in September 1986, to negotiate with the FMLN, with mediation by the Catholic church. Despite Duarte's assurance that El Salvador was seeking a peaceful resolution with the FMLN, the Salvadoran people believed military conflict would be inevitable to end the civil war. In October 1986, a cease-fire with the FMLN was negotiated, but the decree was violated the next month by the Salvadoran government. By 1988, the death toll in El Salvador's civil war totaled more than 60,000. In early 1989, 75 government officials and nine judges resigned because of death threats from the FMLN.

President Cristiani

Alfredo Cristiani Burkard, linked through partisan affiliations with right-wing death squads, took office as president of El Salvador in June 1989, although over 50% of the eligible voters abstained for fear of guerrilla retribution. By September 1989, President Cristiani, with the support of the other Central American leaders, reopened negotiations with the FMLN in Mexico City. Talks were suspended when the Salvadoran army bombed a labor party office on October 31, 1989.

On November 16, 1989, six Jesuit priests, their housekeeper, and her daughter were murdered after nine days of an intense FMLN offensive. In January 1990, President Cristiani admitted that members of the Salvadoran army had been involved in the slaughter. The soldiers involved were charged with the murders.

Also in November 1989, President Cristiani suspended relations with Nicaragua after a plane carrying Soviet-made weapons crashed in El Salvador. The crash was reported to show clearly that Nicaragua was supplying arms to the FMLN. Actually, these reports were a carefully engineered hoax.

Economic Situation

El Salvador is currently undergoing a recession as total debt climbs over $2.2 billion. President Cristiani blames the Duarte regime for El Salvador's fiscal woes. The monumental problem of this unstable economy is the increase in the inflation rate, fueled by depreciation of the colón, high interest rates, and cuts in U.S. aid.

To combat the declining economy, Cristiani has proposed a plan for Economic Reactivation which changed the systems of taxation and exchange rates. Under this plan, the top income tax rate was lowered from 60% to 50%, and various export taxes were abolished. Exchange houses were legalized in hopes of improving the dollar-colón exchange rate. Cristiani's reforms proved very unpopular, especially among those belonging to the lower classes.

Outlook

The United States has declared that it will cut aid to El Salvador in response to their failure to bring Colonel Benavides, a prime suspect in the Jesuit murder case, to trial. Congress will cut aid by 10–30% as a compromise with President Bush, who doesn't want to cut any aid. Cristiani needs to bring all the murderers from the Jesuit case to trial to preserve his credibility. Then he needs to focus on reopening negotiations with the FMLN, whose main demand is that the army be restructured and El Salvador undergo demilitarization.

Sources for More Information

The Central America Fact Book by Tom Barry

NACLA Magazine (Nat'l Conference on Latin America)

Europa World Handbook (Europa Press)

GUATEMALA

Statistics:

Population: 8,700,000 (1988)
Area: 42,042 square miles
Leader: Vinicio Cerezo Arévalo
Principal language: Spanish
Principal religion: Roman Catholicism
GNP: $9.2 billion
Literacy rate: 55% (UNESCO)
Education: secondary enrollment 14%
Average income: $1,120 per capita
Debt: $2.7 billion (1987)

Background

Originally colonized by the Spanish in the 16th century, Guatemala declared its independence from Spain in 1821. With expansive haciendas dotting its countryside, Guatemala gained most of its wealth from agriculture. During the mid-1800's, Guatemala took part in the production and exportation of coffee. This lucrative business created an elite class of extremely wealthy families.

U.S. Intervention

In the early 1900's, the U.S. initially became involved with Guatemala as investors in the banana business. Since then, the U.S. has continued to meddle in Guatemala's internal affairs. In 1904 United Fruit, an American company, was granted 170,000 acres of land for the completion of a trans-Guatemalan railroad by one of their affiliate companies. Within the next few decades, United Fruit quickly became the biggest business in Guatemala. They were granted exemption from taxation, duty-free importation, and a "guarantee of low wages."

In 1944 a popular coalition arose to end the long period of dictatorship. Juan Jose Arevalo was elected to the presidency. He established labor rights and created a state bank to aid small landowners. In 1951 Jacobo Arbenz succeeded Arvelo as president. His Agrarian Reform Law of 1952 specifically targeted the United Fruit Company, which did not cultivate 85 percent of its land. The government expropriated 387,000 acres from United Fruit. Although the government offered to compensate United Fruit for the land based on tax declarations, both United Fruit and the U.S. State Department wanted more.

Immediately following this action, United Fruit launched a campaign to discredit Arbenz. In 1954 the Eisenhower administration approved "Operation Success," a CIA attempt to overthrow Arbenz. Colonel Carlos Castillo Armas overthrew the Arbenz government. Castillo had been trained at the U.S. Command and General Staff School in Fort Leavenworth, and his army had trained on a United Fruit plantation in Honduras. The CIA planned almost every aspect of the coup and provided arms for the rebels. Following the coup, the U.S. poured money into Guatemala to support the Castillo regime.

This U.S.-backed coup ended ten years of political freedom and democracy for Guatemala. A right-wing military dictatorship was reestablished as the primary political force. This system was known especially for "death squads," who assassinated political enemies without a trial.

Opposition

Three junior officers attempted a military coup in 1960 against President Miguel Ydigoras Fuentes, but this rebellion was crushed as U.S.-trained Cuban pilots bombed the rebel-held areas. After several failed coups, in 1982 the four primary guerilla fronts—EGP, ORPA, FAR, and the Guatemalan Labor Party (PGT) —joined together to form a united military front called the Guatemalan National Revolutionary Unity (UNRG).

Popular opposition and unrest grew fast. The people began to form unions and grassroots organizations to oppose the government. In 1972, 60 unions united to form the national Committee of Trade Union Unity (CNUS). In 1978 the Campesino Unity Committee formed, and in 1979 the Democratic Front Against Repression came into being. All of these political fronts and organizations served to exemplify the unrest of the Guatemalan people. With death squads murdering people off the streets, the Guatemalans were essentially prisoners in their own country. In 1981 an estimated 11,000 Guatemalans were killed.

Civilian Constitution

Not until May of 1985, under the leadership of President Mejía Victores, were the Guatemalan people able to secure a civilian constitution. Elections for the presidency, the National Congress, and the 331 mayoralties were held in November 1985. Vinicio Cerezo of the PDCG was elected, and U.S. economic aid was increased and military aid was resumed in support of the new administration.

Death Squads & Violence

In the first six months under President Cerezo, 700 killings were recorded. Cerezo denied that the murders were politically motivated, and he established a government committee to investigate disappearances. He abolished internal departments implicated in political murders, but violence continued unabated.

Reports of right-wing death squad activity resurfaced in mid-1988 as a reaction to the government's increasingly liberal policies. Relations with Mexico became strained as Guatemalan military squads swept through refugee camps in the neighboring country. Amnesty International and the United Nations issued pleas to the Guatemalan government to investigate human-rights abuses.

Continued Instability

Guerilla activity from both the right and left wings escalated in 1989. Cerezo still refused to negotiate with the rebels (UNRG) because of an attempted coup in May 1988. The Guatemalan people became increasingly dissatisfied with the government. Strikes by public-sector workers escalated into full-scale violent confrontations with the Guatemalan military. Terrorist activity, political murders, and rampant human-rights violations continue unchecked.

Political Structure

Guatemala is governed by a unitary republic. The president serves as head of state and is elected by adult suffrage for a non-extendable five-year term. The National Congress is made up of 100 members, of whom 75 are directly elected and 25 are elected by proportional representation. These members are elected every five years and are permitted to be reelected only once. The legal branch is a U.S.-style Supreme Court system. A governmental cabinet is headed and appointed by the president. Elections are held by universal adult suffrage where voting is compulsory for literates and optional for illiterates.

Economic Situation

According to many economists, Guatemala is likely to experience record inflation levels of approximately 60% for 1990. One of the prime reasons for this astronomical rise is the depreciation of the quetzal, Guatemala's unit of currency. Last June, the rate of exchange against the U.S. dollar was Q4.4, which marked a 34% devaluation from the previous year. However, the fall of the quetzal is not the only reason for soaring price rates. The country's enormous deficit and the inability of the government to agree on a budget have also fueled inflation increases.

To combat the troubled economy, the Guatemalans have looked toward commerce. Exports are increasing and becoming more diverse. Within the first four months of 1990, export earnings rose 23.5% as the country continued to expand its U.S. market to not only the traditional exports of sugar, bananas, coffee, and cotton, but also to the nontraditional clothing, vegetables, sesame, and tobacco.

Election of 1990

Guatemala held their second presidential election on November 11, 1990. This was Guatemala's first peaceful transfer of power from one civilian government to another. The election was held to replace President Cerezo, barred by the Guatemalan constitution from serving a second term. General Efrain Rios Monti was disqualified from the election as the former leader of a coup against the Guatemalan government.

The election occurred without incident, although only 57% of eligible Guatemalans voted. No candidate received a majority, so there will be a runoff of the two top candidates, Jorge Serrano Elias and Jorge Carpio Nicolle, on January 6, 1991. Both candidates have similar platforms, although the Stanford-educated Serrano belongs to a Protestant sect, while Carpio is Roman Catholic. Thus, religious issues are expected to play a major role in the January runoff.

Sources for More Information

The Central America Fact Book by Tom Barry
NACLA Magazine (Nat'l Conference on Latin America)
Europa World Handbook (Europa Press)
Central America Newspak (Center for Central America)

HONDURAS

Statistics:

Population: 4,800,000 (1988)
Area: 43,277 square miles
Leader: Rafael Leonardo Callejas
Principal language: Spanish
GNP: $3.3 billion (1986)
Literacy rate: 60% (UNESCO)
Education: secondary enrollment 21%
Average income: $700 per capita
Debt: $3.1 billion (1987)

Background

After the Central American region gained its independence from Spain in 1821, Honduras remained part of the Federal Republic of Central America for 17 years. In 1838 the Republic split and Honduras became an independent nation. Without the benefit of an agro-export economy, Honduras relied primarily on British loans. When President Taft decided that the United States would assume the role as the official debt collector in Central America, the U.S. government positioned itself where it could easily meddle in Honduran politics. Near the turn of the century, Honduras finally began to develop its economy through banana production, with banana companies dominating both the political and economic aspects of the country. These companies controlled the best land in the country, concentrating wealth in the hands of the few.

Political Background

After a shaky political history marked by the rise and fall of numerous governments, Tiburcio Carias Andino emerged as dictator in 1932. During his 16 years of rule, Carias attempted to make Honduras look more like a modern state. Then, during the 1950s, the lower classes began to demand more power. The first successful strike by the banana workers of United Fruit was in 1954. Peasants and workers throughout Honduras began to organize and to demand better wages and agrarian reform. In 1962, President Morales authorized an agrarian reform act, which he approved without review by either United Fruit or the U.S. State Department. In retaliation, United Fruit slowed production and cut jobs, forcing the Honduran government to draft a new, milder reform act which Washington approved.

After deporting thousands of illegal Salvadorans, Honduras entered into a brief one-week war with El Salvador. This war exemplified Honduras' backward state and Honduran officials quickly realized the need to modernize their military and economy. In 1972 General Oswaldo Lopez assumed power, which he lost in 1975 after his foreign minister accepted a $1.25 million bribe from United Brands. General Lopez was replaced by a series of corrupt military juntas.

Intervention from Washington

In 1980, Washington decided it needed a politically secure country bordering troublesome Nicaragua and El Salvador. Thus the U.S. set about "democratizing" the Honduran government. Roberto Suazo Cordova, the Liberal Party's candidate, was elected in 1981. U.S. economic and military aid flowed into Honduras, and Cordova became a convenient extension of Washington. Later in his administration, Cordova took complete control of the political system, including arresting the chief of the Supreme Court and other anti-Cordova justices. The Democratic and Constitutional Coordinator (CODECO) was formed in opposition to the government. The National Party also began opposing the Cordova regime, accusing the government of human rights violations.

General Gustavo Alverez

In December 1982, under the leadership of President Cordova, General Gustavo

Alverez succeeded in amending the Honduran constitution to allow the government less control over the military. Alverez launched a campaign to repress trade unions and left-wing parties, and death squads resurfaced. Throughout 1983, U.S. involvement in Honduras heightened. A U.S. naval base was being constructed at Puerto Castilla, and U.S.-Honduran joint maneuvers were taking place. Meanwhile, the United States was supporting Contras based in Honduras. Alverez was ousted in March 1984, and his successor was General Walter Lopez. The Honduran government responded to growing U.S. opposition by examining its role in U.S. policy, and it suspended U.S. training of Salvadoran troops on Honduran soil.

President Jose Azcona

President Azcona of the Partido Liberal (PL) took office in January 1986. When the Iran-Contra scandal broke into the press, President Azcona requested the withdrawal of the Contra rebels from Honduras. Despite his request, U.S.-Honduran relations remained quite warm. Joint military efforts continued in Honduras throughout 1987, and Honduras received 12 F-5 jets from the United States. In March 1988, Azcona was pressured to request 3,200 U.S. troops after the Nicaraguan army chased a band of Contras into Honduras.

Anti-U.S. Sentiment

Although President Reagan agreed that the U.S. would be responsible for the welfare of the Contras, President Azcona announced that they would have to leave Honduras since they did not have international support. In April 1988, the U.S. extradited a Honduran drug-trafficker in direct violation of the Honduran Constitution. Violent anti-American protests erupted, and a state of emergency was declared in the Honduran capital of Tegucigalpa. In November

1988, Honduras refused to sign a protocol essentially granting the U.S. military free access to Honduran bases.

Human Rights Abuses

Amnesty International reported in 1988 evidence of increased human rights violations by the military and by right-wing death squads. A Honduran human rights organization reported that in 1988 there were 263 "extra-judicial" executions. In January 1989 General Alverez was killed by a left-wing paramilitary group.

New Leadership

On November 29, 1989, Rafael Callejas, the candidate of the right-wing opposition party (PN) was elected president. He identified Honduras' main domestic problems as high unemployment, food shortage, and a fluctuating oil supply. In accordance with an agreement among the five Central American nations, Callejas dispatched the Honduran army to guard Contra encampments. He is actively cooperating with the remaining Central American nations in the repatriation or removal of the Contras from Honduran soil.

Political Structure

The national government of the Republic of Honduras consists of an executive head of state, a national legislature, and a legal system. The president is elected by a general election to serve a four-year term and is responsible for appointing a cabinet of national ministers. The congress, or National Assembly, is comprised of one member and one substitute member elected for every 35,000 people. These legislators are elected by universal suffrage for citizens over 18 years of age. The judicial branch is similar to the United States' Supreme Court system. The Partido Nacional is in power, and the opposition parties are the Partido Liberal, the Partido Innovación y Unidad Social—Social Demócrato (Pinu-SD) and the Partido Demócrata Christiano.

Recession & High Inflation

Like many of its neighboring nations, Honduras has been unable to escape the problem of high inflation. Devaluation of the currency and an increase in sales taxes led to a 35% inflation rate for the first four months of 1990. The government was forced to make drastic budget cuts to counter this rise, but these cuts caused public and private investment to stagnate.

Though 1990 has been a recessionary year, economists are optimistic about growth in 1991. Many incentives have been offered to increase the amount of exports, and this has stimulated commercial production. The government is in the process of securing a $240 million "bridging loan" to improve the Honduran infrastructure.

Outlook

President Callejas' economic reforms appear to be taking effect, amidst continuing death squad activity. Although perhaps economic stability will help in dealing with right-wing death squads, harsh penalties for terrorism and increased government control of the military have yet to be implemented. Callejas also faces grave difficulty in including the large peasant population in his slate of economic reforms—a group he cannot afford to ignore.

Sources for More Information

The Central America Fact Book by Tom Barry
NACLA Magazine (Nat'l Conference on Latin America)
Europa World Handbook (Europa Press)
Central America Newspak (Center for Central America)

textile exports to the U.S. because, in 1989 alone, these taxes cost the country $40 million.

Outlook

Due to the constant threat of political and civil dissonance, President Calderón is having a difficult time maintaining his popularity. He has failed to fulfill many of his campaign promises such as the improvement of the living standards of the poor and reduction of the unemployment rate. According to one survey, 30% of the 1,200 people questioned said they were unhappy within three months under President Arias' (PLN) government in 1986.

Sources for More Information

The Central America Fact Book by Tom Barry

NACLA Magazine (Nat'l Conference on Latin America)

Current History Magazine

Central America Newspak (Center for Central America)

America Magazine

NICARAGUA

Statistics:

Population: 3,745,000 (1989)
Area: 50,200 square miles
Leader: Violetta Barrios de Chamorro
Principal language: Spanish
Principal religion: Roman Catholicism
GNP: $1.6 billion
Literacy rate: 87% (gov't estimate)
Education: secondary enrollment 21%
Average income: $840 per capita
Debt: $6.2 billion (1987)

Background

Originally colonized by the Spanish in 1523, Nicaragua retains a history of U.S.

intervention. U.S. interest in Nicaragua began in the 1830s when a proposal arose to build an interoceanic canal across the country and failed. After President Monroe established the Monroe Doctrine in 1823, the United States considered the Western Hemisphere its exclusive domain. Attempts at communist or socialist government in Central America were considered direct affronts against the United States. This policy extended to the domino theory that if one country in the Western Hemisphere falls to communism, more will topple, and U.S. resources must be committed to prevent such an occurrence.

In 1854, the U.S. warship *Cayne* fired on the port of San Juan del Norte in retaliation for an anti-United States protest. The U.S. military invaded Nicaragua four other times during that decade. In 1912, the U.S. Marines once again invaded. After withdrawing in 1925, the U.S. Army returned one year later to put down an insurgency against the U.S.-backed conservative party. However, the U.S. forces failed and withdrew in 1933. Before leaving, the National Guard, led by Anastasio Somoza, was created to be the U.S. watchdog in Nicaragua. In 1936 Somoza ousted the rightful Nicaraguan leader, and the Somoza family remained in power until 1979.

Sandinistas & Revolution of 1979

In 1979 the Sandinista Front for National Liberation (FSLN) overcame factional rivalries which had plagued the organization since its founding in 1961. With their increased power and unity, the Sandinistas proceeded to overthrow the Somoza government on July 19, 1979. The Sandinista movement is named for Augusto Sandino, who stood up to U.S. policy in Nicaragua. Sandino is a national hero known for his patriotism and ardent nationalism. The most unique feature of the Sandinista Revolution was that it received broad popular support.

The Contras

After the Sandinista victory in 1979, the members of Somoza's National Guard were forced to flee the country because of blatant human-rights violations. Groups of former guardsmen in Honduras created terrorist forces to do battle with the Sandinistas. In 1981, the CIA stepped in and converted these groups into a counterrevolutionary army. These factions were represented by a political umbrella organization known as the FDN. A report by the Council on Hemispheric Affairs condemned the Contras as one of the "worst human-rights violators" in Latin America.

Election of 1984

As part of the Sandinista Revolution in 1979, the leaders promised free elections by 1985. The Sandinistas bettered their claim by holding elections in November 1984, when they received the unquestionable support of the Nicaraguan people in what were called "exemplary" elections by several observers. The FDN withdrew from these elections at U.S. urging. At the time of these elections, United States funding of the Contra (anti-Sandinista) rebels was at its height.

Fall of Contras

After the 1984 election, Congress began to pose serious questions about the role of the Contras. The original justification for Contra funding was to prevent Sandinista shipments of arms to El Salvador. CIA analyst David McMichael publicly revealed these allegations were completely false. All but humanitarian aid was withdrawn, and in 1987, the Iran-Contra affair brought the tale of continued U.S. intervention into the international media. The human-rights violations of the U.S.-backed Contras also began to come to light.

No longer funded by the U.S., the Contras were ousted from Nicaragua

and were reduced to refugees in Honduras. About a year prior to the election of 1990, the plight of the Contras became a serious U.S.-Honduran problem. A host of agreements were made to disarm the Contras and reassimilate them into Nicaragua. With the support of the Bush administration, the Contras rejected the pleas of the Central American leaders and refused to disarm until after the election on February 25.

Election of 1990

The opposition party (UNO) agreed to support Violetta Chamorro as their candidate for president versus the incumbent Daniel Ortega. Ninety percent of all eligible voters registered. Eighty percent of registered voters participated in the election, which was observed by over 2500 foreign observers, including former U.S. President Jimmy Carter. The foreign observers agreed that the Chamorro victory was the result of fair and valid elections. The United States directly funneled $15 million to support the election of Mrs. Chamorro, and it was later revealed by *Newsweek* magazine that the CIA spent $5 million on the election. Mrs. Chamorro was inaugurated on April 25 amid Contra refusals to disarm.

Politics

The political structure of Nicaragua consists of an executive head of state, a national assembly, and legal justices. The president is elected by universal adult suffrage for a period of six years. It is the responsibility of the president to appoint a cabinet and to serve as the commander-in-chief of the armed forces. The national legislature is a 92-member National Assembly. The legal system positions the Supreme Court at the top of the judicial hierarchy, and members of this court are elected for six-year terms by the National Assembly.

There are numerous political parties in Nicaragua. The pro-government party is the National Opposition Union (UNO), which is a compilation of the political groups which oppose the Sandanistan FSLN.

Economic Situation

In recent years, the Nicaraguan economy has been hindered by two devastating phenomena: soaring inflation and an eight-year trade embargo by the United States. Inflation has been fueled by rising world oil prices and drastic shortfalls in crop production. These problems have led to unrest among the citizens. The people demand higher wages, yet the government is cutting the public payroll. This conflict has led to numerous general strikes, the worst of which occurred in July 1990.

The strike involved 85,000 workers and cost roughly $24 million. The strike escalated to such a level that President Chamorro was forced to call on the pro-Sandinista army for help in restoring order. Chamorro made a number of concessions to the workers, including a halt to numerous planned layoffs, a 43% wage increase, and the creation of a joint commission to draft a minimum wage law, none of which have been implemented in the face of worsening poverty, which is likely to cause future strife.

The introduction of a new currency, the *cordoba oro*, has created similar economic problems. The new currency is backed by foreign aid and cutbacks in public spending. Yet, the *cordoba oro* notes are not entering circulation until there are funds to back them. Therefore the old currency will be in circulation simultaneously with the *cordoba oro* for a long time to come.

Outlook

The Chamorro government faces serious difficulties in the months to come. Rampant inflation and other serious economic woes hamper an already crippled balance of trade. The Contra rebels are still a problem, though technically demobilized and disarmed. The standard of living in Nicaragua is in a steady decline, and the pressure to curb that drop will fall squarely on the administration of President Chamorro. The next few months will tell whether the new leader can establish a workable democracy and a competitive economy in Nicaragua.

Source for More Information

The Central America Fact Book by Tom Barry

NACLA Magazine (Nat'l Conference on Latin America)

Journal of Democracy (Nat'l Endowment for Democracy)

Central America Newspak (Center for Central America)

OUR EXPERIENCES WITH THE PUBLIC SERVICE WRITING PROJECT: By Derrick Sung, Lynn Deregowski, Greg Scown

The Project

Our group wrote for the Peninsula Peace and Justice Center under the coordination of Paul George. Our task involved composing "country profiles" for the five major Central American countries: Guatemala, Costa Rica, Honduras, El Salvador, and Nicaragua. The information in these reports was to focus on the political history of each region as well as the U.S. foreign policy and involvement in each of the Central American countries.

Challenges in Completing the Project

Initially, our greatest challenge was developing the correct political "slant" in presenting the information about U.S. involvement in the Central American countries. From Paul George's comments and critiques, it became apparent that the Peace Center expected the reports to be from a rather liberal point of view; however, most of our initial sources were somewhat conservative. This problem motivated us to do extensive research in finding sources with opposing points of view. The final results were reports which we felt were rather objective in their political slant but were still liberal enough to be accepted by the Peace Center.

The extensive research required for this project also posed a challenge to our group. Much of the information needed was either obscure or very recent. Great effort was required to seek out information about the unstable Central American countries in which changes were taking place even as we were compiling our reports.

Our Audience

At the onset of the project, Paul George indicated that our country profiles would be distributed to high school students as well as other affiliated Peace Center members. Thus, we found ourselves writing to two different audiences. We decided to write the reports so that any literate high school student could understand them. The major difference in style between these reports and a paper we would write for an academic class was that these reports were written succinctly and to the point. We were not writing essays to persuade readers to accept a thesis. The country profiles were straightforward presentations of the facts; yet, we presented the facts so that the readers would make their own conclusions about the situations in the countries.

The Learning Experience

Prior to this assignment, none of us had a very thorough understanding of the situation in Central America. Consequently, through our research, all three of us gained a great deal of knowledge about the Central American countries. The information which we acquired was vital to our understanding of current events in the world today.

The experience of writing for the Peninsula Peace and Justice Center was just as valuable as the actual composition of the reports. This project was the first time any of us had had the opportunity to write for a "real life" organization. All of us felt the pressures of a real deadline, but at the same time we knew that we were writing for a purpose. Our final paper would actually be published and put to some use—we were not just writing for a grade. This idea was a great motivating factor as we worked on the project.

Much of what we learned from writing our project could be applied to the more traditional essays in Freshman English. We learned to write from a different, more political point of view. The project was also a good exercise in writing concisely without unneeded phrases or information. This technique is always applicable to any essay. Finally, the research skills which we gained in completing the project apply to any research paper which we may have to write. In fact, because we had to do so much research for this project, we combined this public service project with our freshman research paper.

The Reflective Journal

We did not complete a reflective journal, and none of us feel that such a supplemental assignment would have been necessary or worthwhile. At least once a week, the three of us met outside of class to evaluate and coordinate the progress of our work. In addition, we met with Paul George every two weeks, and he also critiqued and evaluated our project as we completed it. Thus, we had plenty of opportunities to have our project evaluated as we were completing it. Although we do not see the need for a reflective journal, we do feel that it would have been beneficial to have shared more about our progress with our fellow classmates. We would have liked to know more about the other groups in the class and their progress on their individual projects.

Our Project As a Model

Our writing project could be used as a model for any of the public service projects which may involve a reportlike format. One could discuss the effectiveness of our presentation in convincing the readers to draw their own conclusions about the information written. Also, the layout and style of our project could be studied in relation to our intended audience. Of course, with the wide variety of projects available for the public service writings, our composition can only be seen as a small sample of the possible writings which may be done. However, we hope that our project can be looked upon as a successful model for one of the many ways in which the public service writing project can be completed.

SECTION 2: RESEARCH PAPERS

Miami's Dade County Juvenile Justice Center

Dade County Juvenile Justice Center School
3300 N.W. 27th Avenue
Miami, Florida 33142

The mission of Juvenile Justice Center School is to
provide an education pertinent to and compatible with
the capabilities and potential of each student by
focusing on academic and behavioral needs.

We believe that the Juvenile Justice Center School
serves as a link between Dade County Public Schools
and Health and Rehabilitative Services for the
provision of a full-time educational program aimed at
behavior modification, on-phase educational programs,
legal counsel, and custodial care. The Juvenile
Justice Center School realizes that many factors --
social, economic, emotional, and physical -- are
interrelated with the educational factors which join
to make the whole being.

Although we are limited by the transient nature of
our population, we believe that each student has the
inalienable right to be educated. We further believe
that we can serve as a catalyst and help effect a
change in the outlook of some of our students. Time
spent at our school becomes the teachable moment in
which students can become aware of the need to take
responsibility for their lives. We hope to plant a
seed for change by showing students at the Juvenile
Justice Center School that we care about them.

MEET THE AUTHOR PROGRAM

The *Meet the Author Program* was created in 1989 by Professor Joyce Speiller-Morris, who teaches at the University of Miami. Through this program, University of Miami student authors read pieces they have written to various community groups such as the inmates at the Dade County Juvenile Detention Center; residents of a nursing home; a facility for mentally ill adults; a shelter for abused, neglected, and abandoned youth; and teenage gang members. Initially, the *Meet the Author Program* was an entirely volunteer program, with no reward to the students other than the good feeling that comes from giving. The student authors are accompanied by other students from the University of Miami. The students' writings and the ensuing discussion serve as a bridge to various community groups. Often the students are addressing a very different segment of society from their own, but because they have used their writing as a springboard for exposing and exploring their feelings, it enables the audiences to put aside these differences and to likewise reveal their own thoughts and emotions during the discussions. Their writing thus enables students to begin to bridge differences in race, socioeconomic class, nationality, and age.

Since 1982 the *Meet the Author Program* has been incorporated into a service learning course within the Department of English Composition entitled "Writing for and about Community Service." The two essays that follow were written after the students had participated in the *Meet the Author Program* and were taking the service learning course.

Does the Juvenile Justice System Work?

Euclid Zubaran

"All Rise!" Jerome seemed very uninterested as he stood up while the middle-aged man in the robe slowly walked by him as if he were modeling for everyone in the room. Jerome had been picked up by the police last night, just a few blocks from his house. By this time he had watched six cases being tried. Finally, when his name was called, he expertly took a seat between two public defenders. Judge Scott Langley looked through papers, which obviously were Jerome's files. "It says here that you were at Eckerd Youth Development Center in '91. How long were you there for?"

"Eleven months," Jerome replied with a cocky tone of voice.

"You'll be eighteen in March." Jerome nodded. As the Judge raised his head and looked at the boy, he said, "You think it is smart to get picked up for selling crack nine days before your trial for armed robbery?" Jerome ignored his remark as he stared at the desk in front of him. "Well I'll let you go home now, but if you get picked up again before your trial next Friday, you'll be spending a lot of time back there. See you then." Jerome's background exemplifies the position of most juveniles involved in the justice system: the lack of family values and the environment are the factors that keep them in a cycle of crime and punishment.

The majority of the problems facing the kids involved in the criminal justice system can be traced back to the parents, back to the way they have been brought up. They have not developed a sense of empathy, explained Mrs. Rita Logan, a teacher at the Juvenile Justice Center School. According to Mrs. Logan, people usually don't develop a sense of guilt until the age of thirteen. It is not something you are born with, and these kids have not had someone there to tell them not to hit their brother because he is smaller, or to encourage them to share, since most of them come from dysfunctional families. Donald D. Schroeder agrees when he says:

> Vicious criminal behavior occurs in all classes, but is mostly concentrated in inner city ghettos of the United States and other nations where the family structure is most greatly fragmented. . . . more and more youths have little or no compassion, no caring feelings for others but themselves. They feel they become somebody only if they dehumanize another human being. (51)

Some of them probably will never know what guilt is. Mrs. Logan remembers a time she asked a boy who had been involved in the robbery and shooting of an ice cream truck driver this question before the boy was transported to a mental institution: "Don't you feel guilty about the man and his family?" The boy replied, "No. Maybe at this place they will teach me how to feel guilt." It is unreasonable to expect children to learn this feeling on their own, when in a healthy family children learn it from their parents.

Many of the juveniles in the system are very smart, but the lack of encouragement and demand needed to succeed normally provided by the family keeps them in their life of crime. Mrs. Debra Samuels, the librarian at the Juvenile Justice Center School, pointed out a sixteen-year-old boy who had been tested and found to have a very high I.Q. Still, he had been in the detention center several times. He has not had the encouragement and expectations needed to succeed (Samuels interview). The decay in the family unit is partly to blame for the fate of our oncoming generation.

Not only are families responsible for not encouraging juveniles to succeed, but in some cases they encourage them to commit the crimes, explained Debbie Samuels. Their families are in need of the money, so they are encouraged to go out and do whatever it takes to get money (Samuels interview). In cases like this, both the family and the child know that the justice system will only give the child a slap on the wrist (Samuels interview). It is depressing to think that situations like this are going on in the United States today. The system cannot help the kids without the help of the families. Parents need to begin the process by raising their children with moral standards and making sure they develop a sense of empathy, before we can begin to reduce the youth crime rate in the United States.

The environment these individuals live in makes it almost impossible for them to live a crime-free life. A tremendous challenge facing the system is that after the kids are released they are returned to the same environment that caused them to commit the crime. Mrs. Samuels feels that "we are fighting a battle that is almost already lost. . . . All odds are against us." Most of the programs we are implementing today are not working. Kids get arrested over and over again; they even go away for a few months to special programs and a week after being back in their neighborhoods they are back behind bars (Samuels interview). The system as it is being run does not work: it needs to be reformed.

One of the reasons which Rita Logan believes causes the kids to get into trouble in the streets is the fact that they become bored. She believes that crime is exciting for young people. Running from the police is an exciting thing to do, and since these kids don't go to school or work, they have the need for excitement. The excitement of crime leads to the reason behind the need to keep young people busy. If they are in school and working it leaves very little free time to sit around the streets looking for something to do.

The United States has a tremendous problem on its hands—juvenile delinquency. It is getting to the point that the country needs to help these kids for selfish reasons. Crime is on the rise and the potential is there for it to affect everyone.

> Each year, about 700,000 high school students drop out. . . . One out of every four ninth graders will not graduate. . . . Young people under 21 account for more than half of all arrests for serious crimes. . . . During the period 1960–80, arrests of people under 18 for drug abuse increased by an incredible 6000 percent. . . . Only 43 percent of black young people who come from poor homes ever graduate from high school. For whites, the figures is not much better—a graduation rate of only 53 percent. (Kohlberg 132)

The question now is, when is the country going to give the problem priority and really concentrate its efforts to solve it? Clearly the present way to handle it is not an accurate one. The problem is not as important as the solution we need to find. One of the questions Debbie Samuels believes needs to be answered is whether we concentrate our efforts on kids who need a lot of help or whether we spend most of the money on kids who just need a little push to make it.

According to Samuels, a step in the right direction is the Langston Hughes Academy started by Judge Thomas Peterson. When kids are assigned to go to this academy they are required to attend for the whole day. They go to school in the morning, and they have a variety of activities for them to do during the afternoons. This idea of keeping the kids busy keeps them from getting bored, keeps them away from bad influences, and, ultimately, keeps them out of trouble. Another type of program that could be developed is one that not only keeps the kids away from their environment but also takes the place of the traditional family unit, since the families are dysfunctional in these cases. The effectiveness of a program like this will be based on a long-term period, from the time they are sentenced until the completion of high school.

Programs like these can only be possible if the community works hand in hand with the government. The problem needs community service to make a desperately needed difference. There is room for everyone to get involved in schools and academies to which these kids need to be sentenced. "Most of the kids in here," Rita Logan says as she looks around the room as the kids go about their business, "yes, most of them, would be saved if we could send them away. To a military academy or to a boarding school like rich people send their kids. They would only be able to come home on the holidays." Most of them can be saved.

Works Cited

Kohlberg, William H. *Youth Employment Programs Can Reduce Crime*. San Diego: Greenhaven Press, 1989.

Logan, Rita. Personal Interview. December 3, 1992.

Samuels, Debbie. Personal Interview. December 3, 1992.

Schroeder, Donald D. "Lack of Moral Character Causes Crime." San Diego: Greenhaven Press, 1989.

Reach Out

Placement Sheet

Reach Out
CERAS Hall
Stanford, CA 94305

Purpose

Reach Out is a federally funded program designed to provide a variety of academic support services to low-income and/or first-generation college-bound students. The program's goals are to motivate students to attend college, to improve their academic preparation, and to demystify the process of preparing for and applying to college. During the

academic year, Reach Out students receive tutoring
and college counseling and participate in academic
and career workshops on Saturdays throughout the
semester. During the summer, Reach Out offers its
students a six-week residential experience at
Stanford. The program serves East Palo Alto and
Redwood City youth in the Sequoia High School
District.

Writing Task

Write articles for the Reach Out newsletter. Regular
features include profiles of students, profiles of
tutors, and program updates.

Service Learning:
Education with a Purpose

Jeremy Taylor

> We need in education a transformation as far reaching as the one
> which has seized Eastern Europe and what was once the Soviet
> Union, as radical as the abrupt ending of the Cold War, as pro-
> found as the metamorphosis of America's vanquished enemies in
> World War II into its most dependable allies. (Barber 10)

The call to revamp and reform our nation's educational system has been
sounded. The test scores of American high school students are dropping
rapidly while those of Asian and European high school students are improving. Our high school dropout rate is increasing, as is teenage drug abuse and
pregnancy. Today's educators are exploring a variety of alternative learning
approaches. The introduction of community service into the classroom is a
potential solution that is gaining momentum across the country. The successful
integration of a service learning curriculum demonstrates that civic responsibility is fundamental to the advancement of society. Through participation in
community service learning projects, students can begin to better understand
their role in a community and their responsibility to others. The introduction
of community service into the classroom can be a vital part of the restructuring
of our nation's educational goals as well as a valuable tool in teaching social
responsibility.

By combining classroom work with community projects, students are able
to see the applications of their knowledge. Students learn through this method
because they are involved personally with the outcome; they do not have to

feel like passive bystanders. This approach bring a sense of purpose back to education. Presently, classrooms are filled with students asking questions such as "Why do I need to learn this?" and "When am I ever going to use that?" Participating in service learning experiences in the "real world" helps students to begin to find some answers to these challenging questions. As students realize that knowledge gained through regular course work and classroom learning can be applied outside the classroom, they become more motivated.

Application of community service as a way to enhance and invigorate the learning process is supported at many levels. After the passage of the landmark Community Service Act of 1990, Senator Edward Kennedy explained why he supports service learning:

> Service learning should be a central component of current efforts to reform education. There are few better ways to inspire a child's interest in science than by allowing him or her to analyze and clean a polluted stream. There are few better ways to help a student's grammar than by having him or her tutor a recent immigrant learning to speak and write English. (772)

Along with Senator Kennedy, students, administrators, and teachers all over the country are realizing the value of service learning. When students see their knowledge promoting the growth of the community, their degree of knowledge retention is increased. A sixteen-year-old member of an ambulance crew says:

> In school you learn chemistry and biology and stuff and then forget it as soon as the test is over. Here you've got to remember it because somebody's life depends on it. (Conrad 745)

In addition to increasing learning retention, studies show that students who participate in community service learning experiences develop a more positive attitude toward others as well as a higher sense of self-esteem; they also have fewer disciplinary problems (Conrad 747). Most importantly, working with others on community service projects can increase students' motivation to learn. Teacher Don Zwach of Waseca, Minnesota, who incorporates community service into his curriculum, points to the significant impact that community service projects have had on his students' motivation:

> This is the most enthusiastic class I've had in thirty years. You hear a lot about the problems of motivating students in the 1990s. But there's absolutely no problem motivating these young people. (Kilsmeier 741)

Other teachers report that their academic goals are much more easily accomplished when students apply their knowledge to situations outside of the classroom. For example, after tutoring third and fourth graders, seventeen-year-old Quinn Hammond said, "This taught me to have more patience and gave me a real good feeling. Volunteering gave me a respect for teachers" (Kilsmeier 741).

Opponents of civic learning hold to the belief that the purpose of an educational system is to educate, not to teach civic responsibility. They claim that an academic institution has no right to coerce students into a service behavior.

Benjamin Barber captures the limitation of such "academic purism" in his new book, *An Aristocracy for Everyone,* when he says that these educators believe in learning "not for career, not for life, not for democracy, not for money; for neither power nor happiness, neither career nor quality of life, but for its own pure sake" (203).

While the debate on whether to include community service in the academic curriculum grows more intense, this method of education through service is not new. When America's first colleges were established in the seventeenth and eighteenth centuries, service was one of their fundamental values and goals; they structured curricula to support their belief in service to the church, service to the local community, and service to the emerging nation. In fact, Rutgers University was chartered in 1766 to promote "learning for the benefit of the community" (Barber 246).

From 1766 to the present many approaches and opinions have been offered on the subject of education through community service. Today's proponents work with ideas that are similar to those of John Dewey. In *Experience and Education,* published in 1913, Dewey developed the idea of stimulating academic achievement through actions directed toward others. Dewey spent much of his life trying to bring education and experience together in order to promote democracy as a "way of life and not just a political system" (Barber 247). When Woodrow Wilson assumed the office of President, he encouraged a renewed interest in civic responsibility and service learning:

> . . . as a nation we are becoming civically illiterate. Unless we find better ways to educate ourselves as citizens, we run the risk of drifting into a new kind of Dark Age. (qtd. in Barber 247)

In the 1950s, after the "Dark Age" of education during World War II, a new approach to civic education, the Citizenship Education Project, was developed by teachers from Columbia University. This program urged community involvement and participation and also contained the famous "Brown Box" with hundred of ideas for community interaction (Conrad 744). The 1970s brought another new wave of reports condemning the passivity of our school systems. The National Committee on Secondary Education, the Panel on Youth of the President's Science Advisory Committee, and the National Panel on High School and Adolescent Education all supported the integration of education into the community (Conrad 744). By the mid-1980s, several pilot programs had been initiated, and community service programs began to appear in classrooms throughout the nation.

These historical facts provide a background for the educational innovations of the 1990s, and perhaps the most important step in the integration of public service into the classroom: the National and Community Service Act of 1990, passed by the Congress of the United States, will provide funding for community service programs from kindergarten through college. It is the most thorough community service bill ever passed. The legislation provided federal appropriations of $62 million in 1991, $95.5 million in 1992, and will provide $105 million in 1993 for community service programs. A major goal of this program is to inspire interest in community service at a young age. Senator Edward Kennedy hopes that "by teaching young children to help others, we will also be encouraging the values that will help keep America strong for the next generation" (772).

Academic communities all over the country are beginning to realize the value of community service, and more programs are being introduced at the high school and college level. For example, service programs have been developed in Washington and Vermont. One program in particular, PennSERVE, developed in Pennsylvania, is achieving incredible success. PennSERVE emphasizes the link between the classroom and community service. Because of PennSERVE, the number of schools offering academic credit for service has doubled in two years, and community service has become a common topic of debate (Briscoe 760). PennSERVE is just one of the many programs which has grown and flourished since the passage of the Community Service Act of 1990.

I was introduced to service learning through another type of program, a Community Service Writing Project; my experiences have been both memorable and beneficial. I chose to be placed in a Community Service English class because I had become bored with "regular" English, which I characterize as writing solely to please my teacher and receive a good grade. I looked forward to an English class with a bit of a twist, one that would expose me to community service in my first year of college. Through my English class, I decided to work at a public service organization that helped disadvantaged youth from nearby high schools prepare for college.

Along with four other students, I met with the organization's leader and discovered how our skills were to be utilized. Our group was to be responsible for developing a newsletter for prospective students and their parents. The newsletter was to include articles highlighting various aspects of the organization, so each person in our group wrote on a different topic. I chose to interview a new staff member, a classmate interviewed students who were involved with the program, and another group member researched the organization's incentive program to learn about how it rewarded students for their academic achievement.

While my finished product was less than a full page of text, the "behind the scenes" work was immeasurable and invaluable. I learned "real-life" skills while completing this project. First, I had to research the organization to prepare for my interview. It was then necessary to formulate questions for the interview and decide what my focus was going to be. During the interview I discovered how interviewing is an art and realized the difficulty of "staying on track" and directing the conversation toward key points. After the interview, it was necessary to review my notes, determine the focus of my article, and decide what information to include and what to leave out. Finishing this process, I wrote a draft and turned it in to the organization. In an English class, after one turns in a paper the process is ended; this was not the case with my interview. The leader of the organization requested that I write another draft with a slightly different focus. While this was a new situation for me, I approached it as a challenge. Complying with the leader's suggestions,

I wrote a revised article which addressed the issues she saw as important. This draft received approval to be placed in the newsletter and brought my writing project to a conclusion.

Although this project was lengthy, and, at times, frustrating, it was an invaluable experience. I was refreshed writing with a purpose other than to receive an "A" while knowing that my writing would be read by someone other than a professor. I felt a strong sense of responsibility to my organization, and I wanted to produce something of which I would be proud. But the writing was just a part of the overall experience; this project introduced me to people, to ideas, and to situations that I would not have experienced in the classroom. It gave me a sense of pride and illustrated that I am able to reach out to people in different ways and through different mediums. I would not trade my "real-life" experiences while working on this project for any other kind of essay assignment. Through my interaction with the organization and its members, I feel that in a subtle way this project has prepared me to participate more effectively in society.

In the early eighties, Ernest Boyer and Fred Hechiner asked that "a new generation of Americans . . . be educated for life in an increasingly complex world . . . through civic education [that] prepares students of all ages to participate more effectively in our social institutions" (Barber 248).

Today we stand at a crucial juncture; we can initiate plans to forge ahead into the future, or we can continue to be satisfied with the status quo. Just as the world is changing around us, our educational system must change to meet the needs of today's students. The integration of civic education is an important part of that change. Community service, by showing us that we all have the means to contribute, can be the critical step in producing citizen graduates, graduates who realize their social responsibility and who will participate more effectively in our social institutions. Times have changed, yet our academic institutions have remained the same. The call for change has been sounded. It won't fade away; it will only grow louder.

Works Cited

Barber, Benjamin R. *An Aristocracy of Everyone: The Politics of Education and the Future of America.* New York: Ballantine, 1992.

Briscoe, John. "PennSERVE: The Governor's Office of Citizen Service." *Phi Delta Kappan.* June 1991: 758–760.

Conrad, Dan, and Diane Hedin. "School-Based Community Service: What We Know from Research and Theory." *Phi Delta Kappan.* June 1991: 743–749.

Kennedy, Edward M. "National Service and Education for Citizenship." *Phi Delta Kappan.* June 1991: 771–773.

Kielsmeier, Jim and Joe Nathan. "The Sleeping Giant of School Reform." *Phi Delta Kappan.* June 1991: 739–742.

SECTION 3: REFLECTIONS ON SERVICE LEARNING

Conservation Club at the University of Northern Iowa

Placement Sheet

The Conservation Club, a student organization at the University of Northern Iowa, makes students more aware of the environment. The goals of the club are to show students the steps all people can take to improve the quality of the environment. The Conservation Club meets monthly.

The Conservation Club sponsors a campuswide "recycle day" each semester, where they help gather the community's recyclable materials.

Writing activities include making "awareness flyers" or a calendar of events. Jennifer Hancock decided to use the idea of awareness flyers to promote a specific "issue of the week." These flyers were placed in all the buildings around the campus.

JOURNAL: By Jennifer Hancock

Oct. 13
   I lost my other notebook that had my journal in it so this is my new one. By keeping it on computer, I won't have to worry about losing this one.

Oct. 15

Today I decided to change my topic to the reclamation of land which has been strip-mined. I became interested in the topic during the summer because I worked for a construction and mining company and knew that the subject was of great concern to it. I also plan on majoring in environmental planning and minoring in geology so I think the topic will be interesting to research.

Oct. 18

I still haven't heard from the Sierra Club so I have decided to change my community service organization to U.N.I.'s Conservation Club. I am interested in the workings of the club and support its efforts to make a change in the environment by educating the community. I began my research on the land reclamation and seem to have found several sources.

Oct. 20

After class today I went to the library to try to do a little more research. Later I called Genevieve Burke of the Conservation Club but she was not home. I left a message for her to call and explained a little bit about who I was.

Oct. 21

Genevieve Burke returned my call and said she was sure the club could find something for me to write for them. I had heard from one of my geology professors that the president of the Conservation Club was in several classes at Latham Hall, which is where I spend most of my time for labs. I think that it will be easier to meet with him because of this and also found out that he lives in my dorm. This will make it easier to find a time to meet with him because I have a hard time finding a time during the day when I'm not either in one of my labs or working.

Oct. 25

I spoke with Scott today about the writing for the Conservation Club and he had several ideas for me to choose from. I decided to do weekly flyers. He gave me complete freedom in what I wanted to do for the flyers but suggested that I could do an environmental "issue of the week." He said the flyers would be a good

idea because he had very little free time to help me
with this; the only thing I needed to do was have him
look over the flyers when I was done to make sure I was
not sending out inaccurate information under the name
of the Conservation Club.

Oct. 27
   I did some more research on my report today and am
   running into the problem of not finding up-to-date
   information. I have also written to the mining company
   I worked for this summer to see if they could send me
   any information about strip mining and the reclamation
   of the land afterward. My professors in the geology
   department have promised to give me any information on
   the subject if they see it. I found some information
   for my environmental issues of the week while I was
   researching my topic.

Oct. 31
   Today I worked on my environmental issue of the week
   for the Conservation Club. I'm getting my information
   from the Capstone classes and still trying to narrow
   down the list of issues I want to cover to four. It's
   difficult because I don't want to talk above my
   audience, but at the same time I want to capture their
   attention and make them take a new look at their
   actions. I'm really starting to get into this idea; I
   would feel as if I accomplished my goal if the flyers
   made people change even a little aspect of their lives
   to help preserve the environment. The idea I am hoping
   to get across to them is that if everyone put even a
   little effort into protecting the environment, the task
   would not seem impossible. I am leaning toward
   wildlife and deforestation for my first two flyers. I
   feel that both of these are important issues that
   everyone will be able to relate to and make some change
   in their life to improve the situations of both.

Nov. 1
   I made a little progress on my research paper today.
   I'm trying to find the way I would like to organize my
   paper, which I have always had a little trouble with.
   There's a program on my computer which I'm trying to
   learn so that I can use the note cards on it to
   organize my sources for the bibliography of my paper.

I seem to be having a little difficulty with it but hopefully I'll master it soon.

Nov. 3

The first two flyers seem to be coming along nicely. I decided on a format which tells a little bit about the problem with a few short facts. Then, in order to relate the issue to everyday situations, I listed ways for people to make small changes in their lives which would add up to make a big difference in the preservation of the environment. I tried to suggest ideas other than the obvious ones like just recycling. It was surprising for me to learn how many things I do that harm the environment. If nothing else comes out of this project, at least I've found myself making positive changes in my life which will help the environment instead of harming it.

Nov. 5

I wrote the first two pages of my research paper today, and though it is very rough, I am starting to see how it will end up. I still haven't heard back from Kiewit Construction Company, so I need to find some more sources of information for my paper. Hopefully my writing buddy will be able to suggest some to me.

Nov. 8

My writing buddy is now another person from the class instead of Kara Jane. She called today to make an appointment for Wednesday around 4:00 to look over the first two to five pages of my paper. I also have an appointment with Dr. Butler-Nalin at 9:45 on Wednesday to discuss my writings for the Conservation Club. I'm going to try to meet with Scott VenderHart on Thursday or Friday to show him what issues I have done and see if he has any more suggestions.

Nov. 10

Today I met with Dr. Butler-Nalin to discuss my community service writing. She seemed to like the progress I had made on it and offered a few suggestions on word changes. She didn't make any drastic changes, which pleased me. They seem to be effective flyers and I am anxious to see them in print. I made the revisions she suggested and started work on the other two flyers. I chose to write about the atmosphere and energy conservation. Hopefully they will be done by next week and I can show them all to Scott at once. He seems to be short on time so I think this will work out better than several short meetings with him. I had to reschedule my meeting with Julie because I had a lab that I had to go to at the last minute. We rescheduled for Thursday night at 8:30.

Nov. 11

I met with Julie tonight to show her the first couple of pages of my paper. She made a few suggestions on how to improve it, but basically, since it was only a rough draft (and my rough drafts are very rough until I go back to fill in the holes), she couldn't make many suggestions that I didn't already know how to take care of. We did make an appointment for Tuesday so she could show me how to use the CD-ROM at the library, though. Hopefully that will give me the sources I'm having trouble finding for the land reclamation part of the paper.

Nov. 15

Today in class I made an appointment for Friday with Dr. Butler-Nalin to discuss my environmental issues again. She also told us that the first eight pages of our research paper were due on Wednesday. This is going to be a little difficult for me since most of the work I have been doing has been for the community service project and not the paper, but I'm not too far behind so I'm sure I'll be able to get it done.

Nov. 16

I went to the library to meet Julie but I didn't see her or at least didn't recognize her. I also spent a couple of hours working on the paper for class on Wednesday. Scott said he would be free to meet with me tomorrow at 5:30 to look over the issues before I turned them in to Dr. Butler-Nalin. Because I didn't see Julie at the library, Randy Riewerts showed me how to use the CD-ROM. I found some more sources, but the more up-to-date ones were gone, so I'll go back later this week to see if they have been returned.

Nov. 17

I turned in my first eight pages of the paper today and made some revisions on the rough drafts of my

environmental issues before I showed them to Scott. He
seemed pleased with how I set them up, and the information I used was accurate, so he had no problem with
them as far as that was concerned. He did want my deforestation flyer to focus on the deforestation in the
United States and not so much on the South American
rain forests, though. I'll do some more research on
that tomorrow and have a new rough draft of that one on
Friday for Dr. Butler-Nalin.

Nov. 19

I had some problems with my printer so I was late to my
meeting this morning, but I still got to meet with Dr.
Butler-Nalin. She looked over my issues and suggested
a change of wording on one of the flyers, but nothing
major was changed on any of them. She did suggest,
however, that I should enlarge the issue that I was
focusing on for the flyer because it was not catching
the audience's attention the way I wanted it to. After
I left her office I made the changes right away so that
I could finish up the flyers and focus on my paper for
the rest of the semester.

Environmental Issues

Jennifer Hancock

ENVIRONMENTAL ISSUE OF THE WEEK: DEFORESTATION

In 1990, nearly 74 percent of the Forest Service budget was devoted directly or
indirectly to the sale of timber, whereas only 4 percent of the budget was used
for recreation, 2.3 percent for wildlife and fish conservation, and 1.3 percent for
soil, water and air management. Today an estimated 95 percent to 97 percent
of the country's virgin forests have been cleared away and what remains is
under threat. These forests are disappearing at a much higher rate than the
tropical rain forests in Brazil. At current rates of logging, all unprotected ancient forests in western Washington and Oregon will be gone by the year 2023.

What Can You Do?

- Plant trees on a regular basis in your town and around your home and
  take care of them so they survive.

- Reduce your use of the wood and paper products you don't really need, recycle the paper products you do use, and buy recycled products.
- Pressure your school to buy recycled paper products.
- Recycle aluminum cans, or even better, switch to reusable glass containers. Buying aluminum products encourages the development of more aluminum mines in the Amazon basin which are powered by dams. These dams flood large areas of the tropical rain forests.
- Reduce your consumption of beef, some of which is raised by clearing of tropical and other forests.
- Avoid cutting trees at Christmas; instead, buy a living tree in a tub which you can later plant outdoors.
- Help restore a degraded forest in an area near your home.

ENVIRONMENTAL ISSUE OF THE WEEK: ENERGY

The United States is the world's greatest energy user and waster; at least 43 percent of all energy used in the United States is needlessly wasted. That waste equals the total amount of energy consumed by two-thirds of the world's population. Americans have one-third of the world's automobiles and drive about as many kilometers in one year as the rest of the world combined. One-fifth of the electricity produced in the United States is used for lighting, which is equivalent to the output of 100 large power plants. About one-third of all the electricity produced in the United States is used to power household appliances. Our current dependence on nonrenewable fossil fuels is the primary cause of air and water pollution, land disruption, and global warming.

What Can You Do?

- Use natural lighting whenever possible.
- Walk or ride a bicycle for short trips.
- Car pool or ride mass transit systems as much as possible.
- Use ceiling fans and small floor fans to eliminate or reduce the use of air conditioners.
- Close windows and drapes on sunny days and open them on cold days and at night.
- Use less hot water by taking 2- to 5- minute showers instead of baths, wash dishes only with full loads, wash clothes in warm or cold water, and don't let water run while bathing, shaving, brushing teeth, or washing dishes.
- Disconnect air conditioners at the circuit breaker during winter—otherwise a small heater in the compressor runs year-round.
- Use the sun or air to dry clothes instead of electric clothes dryers.

ENVIRONMENTAL ISSUE OF THE WEEK: THE ATMOSPHERE

NASA estimates that the annual level of stratospheric ozone over heavily populated areas has decreased at twice the rate scientists predicted only a few years ago. Chlorofluorocarbons released into the lower atmosphere are drifting into the upper atmosphere and are depleting ozone faster than it is being formed. The thinner ozone layer allows more ultraviolet radiation from the sun to reach Earth's surface. Scientists predict that the current rate of depletion will cause devastating effects, such as an extra 12 million cases of skin cancer within the next 30 years, sharp increases in eye cataracts, decreased yields in important food crops, and suppressed human immune systems which would have an effect similar to the AIDS virus.

What Can You Do?

- Avoid purchasing products which contain chlorofluorocarbons, carbon tetrachloride, and methyl chloroform.
- Stop using all aerosol spray products. Even those which don't contain CFCs and HCFCs emit propellant chemicals into the air. Use roll-on and hand-pump products instead.
- Buy only fire extinguishers which use dry chemicals.
- Check your car's air conditioner to be sure it is not leaking, since leaky air conditioners in cars are the single largest source of CFC emissions in the United States.
- Pressure legislators to require that all products which contain or require CFCs, halons or other ozone-depleting chemicals during their manufacture be clearly labeled so that consumers can consciously choose whether or not to purchase these products.
- Don't smoke, or smoke outside or in a closed room vented to the outside.

ENVIRONMENTAL ISSUES OF THE WEEK: WILDLIFE

Each year, up to 50,000 species of wildlife become extinct. People cause most of these extinctions through activities such as deforestation, desertification, and destruction of wetlands and coral reefs. If these activities continue at their present rates, an estimated 500,000 species will become extinct.

What Can You Do?

- Support efforts to reduce testing on animals to a minimum and to humanely treat the ones which are tested.
- Spay or neuter your dogs or cats. Overpopulation leads to the destruction of over 15 million unwanted pets each year, which is 75 times the number of dogs and cats killed each year for research and teaching purposes.

- Do not buy exotic pets such as fish or birds imported from tropical or other areas. One or more animals die for each one that actually reaches the pet store and most of the pets that do make it to the stores die prematurely.
- Purchase only cans of tuna which are caught by dolphin-safe methods.
- Pressure elected officials to pass laws requiring larger fines or longer sentences for wildlife poachers and to provide more personnel for wildlife protection.
- Reduce habitat destruction and degradation by recycling; better yet, reuse items and reduce your use of throwaway items.

Bay Area Action

Placement Sheet

Bay Area Action
Palo Alto, CA
Contact Person: Volunteer Coordinator
Hours: 10-6 M-F

Purpose

Bay Area Action works locally to achieve the Earth Day "Agenda for the Green Decade," preserving biological diversity, reducing waste, using water wisely, creating a safe, sustainable energy system, preserving the climate and atmosphere, and stabilizing population growth.

BAA's projects use many strategies -- hands-on restoration work, developing school curricula, neighborhood organizing, work place environmental audits, rallies, video presentations, publications, and sales of environmentally sound products -- but they all serve one goal: to develop a network of well-informed activists in the Bay Area.

Writing Opportunities

Research and write articles about the controversial land issues concerning Saint Patrick's (Menlo Park) or San Bruno Mountain (San Bruno); for example, do an economic analysis of the effects of keeping the acreage as open space versus [housing] development.

Write articles for BAA's newsletter on such topics as the organizing process for this year's Earth Day.

Document the work of BAA programs; conduct interviews and research BAA files to learn about current projects, and write clear summaries describing the projects and explaining their value. These will be used to help new volunteers familiarize themselves with the agency and as a resource for grant writers.

Assist the Volunteer Coordinator in drafting grant proposals, requesting funds to support BAA programs or to purchase a computer. Past proposals and a grant writing handbook are available for your use.

Bay Area Action is an active organization, and new writing needs continually arise; consult with the Volunteer Coordinator about current projects.

Reflections

Justin Augustine

It was sometime in early June. I was hastily filling out my CIV and English preference forms, not really giving either of them much of a thought. I had just graduated and anything that resembled schoolwork totally turned me off. The statement on the sheet in front of me read, "Check this box if you would like to be placed in a course that has a community service writing component." I went ahead and checked the box, although I'm really not sure why. But I did. And now I'm grateful.

I feel that the Community Service Writing Project is an integral part of the Stanford writing curriculum. A university should not be separate from the community in which it resides, but rather a vital part of it. The Community Service Writing Project accomplishes that task by connecting Stanford with the community of Palo Alto and the Bay Area. Before I began the project, I rarely left campus and knew almost nothing concerning the community of Palo Alto. I'll admit that my particular project didn't require that I journey off campus, but it did force me to become aware of my new community and its environmental concerns.

Bay Area Action was the organization I worked with. Located in the community of Palo Alto, Bay Area Action is a nonprofit organization whose goal is to educate the public concerning environmental topics. Its tool in accomplishing that goal is a newsletter which is published quarterly. When I met with Bay Area Action's Volunteer Coordinator, she mentioned several topics which needed to be publicized: a polluted watershed, development in Menlo Park, and the plight of the California tiger salamander. It quickly became obvious that she really wanted an article concerning the salamanders, and so, when I left our meeting, my task was to write an informative article on them for the Bay Area Action newsletter.

Write a paper, get a grade, write a paper, get a grade, write a paper, get a grade. Throughout high school that is what my writing classes consisted of. The Community Service Writing Project put an end to that monotonousness. It added a new dimension to my writing. People. Real people would be reading this article. I wasn't just writing for a grade or to please myself. Now others, besides myself and a teacher, were going to really care about what I had to say and how I said it. I was writing to convey a message to an entire community. They're not grading me, they want to learn from me. Realizing that pumped some extra adrenaline through my body, and I knew that I really wanted to make this paper a success. My article was going to be published. There would be no grading scale. My purpose now was to communicate ideas successfully to the people who would be reading the newsletter.

For a moment that thought intimidated me. Throughout high school, it seemed that no matter what I wrote, I always received the same grade. As a result, I became apathetic toward formal writing and believed that no matter how hard I tried I would always receive the same grade. Initially, my attitude toward the Community Service Writing Project was the same, and I said to myself, "I'm not a very good writer. How am I going to please a whole community when I can't even please one teacher?" Instead though, the Community Service Writing Project gave me a new perspective and also confidence. I turned that statement in my head around and said, "If I can please a whole community, then in the future pleasing one teacher won't seem nearly as difficult." That thought, too, pumped more adrenaline through my body and made me want to succeed all the more.

The idea of service also contributed to my desire to succeed. The Community Service Writing Project was very similar to other volunteer tasks I had performed in the past. During high school I volunteered at my community's recycling center. It was a pain to wake up every other Saturday morning at 7:30 and then work for five hours sorting and cleaning dirty, sticky beer and pop cans. But when I was finished each Saturday, I always felt good because I knew I had worked hard and had contributed to both my community and the environment. Never once did I regret dragging myself out of bed and volunteering my labor. It's the same with this project. Researching the information and writing about it required a lot of time and hard work—just like waking up early on those Saturdays and working for five hours straight. But now that I'm done with the paper, I'm thankful I made the efforts that I did. I'm honestly proud of the final product and believe that it will provide its reader with an excellent background and understanding of the California tiger salamander. And the more people who read the article, the more educated this community will be in making environmental decisions in the future—definitely a service.

Together, those two experiences have convinced me that volunteerism is part of life. It isn't just something you do in high school so you can put it on your college transcript. It is something you do your whole life because you enjoy contributing to a cause in which you believe, and you enjoy the satisfaction of helping others. Trite as it may sound, it felt good to know that my efforts were helping to protect the environment and the future well-being of its inhabitants. With the Community Service Writing Project, the satisfaction came from the fact that my writing was being used for a positive purpose, in this case, educating the public. And that's what volunteerism is about—performing a service for others and receiving satisfaction as pay.

I said before that I don't know why I checked that box on the English preference forms. To be honest, I think I do. I wanted something new and different. I wanted to learn. And I wanted to continue that feeling of pride you achieve after working hard and receiving no pay except for the knowledge that you have contributed to a job well done. And while on that hot summer day in June my thoughts may not have been concentrating on what the box really meant, something inside of me did. Some inner conscience felt that down the road I'd appreciate checking that box. That inner conscience was right.

Vitas Health Care Corporation of Florida

Room 653

Lam Nguyen

Room 653: it's a nice room with sky-blue walls bordered by a soothing pastel pink trim up near the ceiling. Thin peach-colored curtains hang from the large window transforming the harsh intruding sunlight into a soft glow of warmth. But none of this matters to the man inside the room. His presence breaks the tranquility purposely set there to calm him. Lying there in a sterile hospice bed, futilely battling a disease that has already wasted away his body, he reaches out to touch my hand. I take his fragile, bony hand, and not really knowing what to say I try my best to soothe his agitation. I learned earlier that he was brought to the AIDS Hospice because he needed to be stabilized and right now all I wanted to do was to see him get better. I returned a few days later to find him in much better shape. He introduced himself as Achilles and we talked for a while. Before I left him that afternoon he had promised me that if I came the next day, he would get out of his bed and walk for me.

And so the next day I went to the Hospice with a mango in my hand (he and I were going to share his most favorite fruit as a victory celebration for getting up to walk) only to find Room 653 empty. The bed was still there and so were the curtains and everything else except for Achilles. Well, I thought, maybe he walked without me, so I went looking for him. And when I couldn't find him I went to the office. I'm sorry, but Achilles passed away last night. What? Impossible. This must be a mistake; I just saw him yesterday. He promised he would walk for me. See? I brought him this mango. See?

But that was last week. And now I visit Sammy in Room 653. He lies in the same bed as Achilles had, in the same sky-blue room with the same peach curtains. And dying too of the same disease. It's not easy. It's not easy volunteering in an AIDS hospice where people go either to die or to receive critical stabilization. But it's worth it. A volunteer gains just as much or even more than the patient by giving some of his compassion and love to those who so desperately need it.

And among those who most desperately need love and compassion are those at an AIDS hospice. Hospice is "a specialized health care program emphasizing the management of pain and other symptoms associated with terminal illness . . . designed especially to help patients and their families face the physical, emotional, social, financial and spiritual aspects of their lives and the patient's death" (Vitas 3). The hospice views death as a natural process and does not hasten nor postpone it. The primary goal of the hospice is to let the patient die full of dignity and free of pain. My role as a volunteer at the South Miami AIDS Inpatient Unit or Hospice is to visit the patients and just be their friend. I listen to what they have to say, whether it be about their worries or about the weather. My job is to let them know they have a friend they can always talk to and that someone out there cares for them. The social support that many people dying of AIDS find lacking, I try to help provide.

I, personally, have grown and learned so much from volunteering at the AIDS Hospice. Volunteering is no doubt a two-way street, especially in the case of an AIDS hospice. For one thing, the required fourteen-hour training period expanded my knowledge of the disease itself and how it affects the patient and family. The sessions banished most of the ignorance I held when it came to AIDS and AIDS patients. I learned things about AIDS that I would not have known if not for volunteering. Issues such as the diseases related to AIDS, the medications used for them, and psychological factors involved were all covered in these sessions.

I believe volunteering can greatly affect the volunteer in that it gives him the feeling that he can make a difference in the world around him. It is a wonderful feeling to know that I can reach out to another person and really make a difference in his life, no matter how small or insignificant the change.

Whenever I visit a patient at the Hospice and can make him laugh or just get it through to him that people out there really do care what happens to him, I feel that I've made his life that little bit better. Volunteers have the power to change another person's life, and the realization of that fact can in turn change the volunteer for the better.

Volunteerism's worst enemy is Selfishness. Too many people are self-centered and just plain selfish. They care only for what directly affects themselves and are involved with their own singular problems. What a volunteer does is involve himself with the problems of the world. By volunteering, I became aware of other people around me. By seeing the problems of other people, I can put myself and the world in the right perspective. I've changed my own perspective since volunteering at the Hospice. I can see now that I'm not the only one with hardships and, in fact, my own problems are minimal compared with what those at the Hospice have to face every day. I have become more aware of other people and can empathize with them much more easily because of volunteering. Many of my own views have been altered because of the volunteering experience. After seeing some of the emotional and physical suffering these people have to endure, I realize how fortunate I am and that I should not take what I have for granted.

One big impact volunteering at the AIDS Hospice had on me was the issue of death. After the initial shock of Achilles' death, I realized how sudden and unexpected death could be. In my mind, I couldn't accept the fact that I just saw him and the next night he dies. I kept saying to myself, "But I just saw him." Finally, having now accepted his death, I realize how precious life really is.

Achilles' death also showed me something I never saw before: my own inner strength. I had met Achilles' friend of ten years at the Hospice in one of my earlier visits. He called me the day after Achilles' death. It was very difficult to talk with him because of the pain and grief he felt over the death. He would break out in a crying fit, and it was an intensely painful experience to hear him suffer for his lost friend. But I knew he needed to talk it out, and he called me for relief, so I tried my best to comfort him. By the end of our conversation he thanked me for listening and I realized something about myself. I recognized within myself a strength that I never saw before. He needed someone to lean on and I was there for him. I know now that I do have an inner anchor that will keep me from floating away when times get rough. I don't think that realization would have been possible if not for my volunteering.

When I asked the Director of Volunteers and Bereavement Services for Vitas AIDS Hospice, Ibiset Salinas, who she thought benefited more from volunteering—the volunteer or the patient—she replied, "The most obvious benefit of volunteering is to the patient. He is the one in need of help and the volunteer fulfills that need . . . but you cannot ignore the fact that the volunteer will be affected. A volunteer will go through all the ups and downs of life with the patient and experience a different life through the eyes of the patient. Those experiences are what the volunteer will take with him after he is finished, . . . experiences that can change a volunteer."

I agree completely with Ibiset's statement. Volunteering will help those in need but that same act of giving will also come back to the volunteer. Achilles is gone now and for what little comfort I gave him, in return he has given me an awareness about myself and others around me. Through volunteering I have dispelled my own ignorance about AIDs and the people infected with it. I have also realized that within me is the potential for change. By going "hands-on" with the real world, I now have a small sense of the people around me and where I stand in this new perspective. I know now through my own solidarity and willingness to help others, I can make a difference, for the better, in other people and the world.

And so in that quiet room of 653 I will continue to visit and befriend anyone in need of some company. Right now it's Sammy, but I know not for long. Soon another will reside within the sky-blue walls of 653 to replace the space that Sammy and before him, Achilles, once held. But no matter who it is, he will still need the comfort and assurance of a friend. And that friend will be me.

Works Cited

Salinas, Ibiset. Personal interview. 5 December 1992.
Shaw, Tonya. *Vitas: Innovative Hospice Care Training Manual*. May 1992.

Appendix

Quilt made by Anne Takemoto, Jackie Schmidt-Posner, and students. (*Photo courtesy of Urender Shaw.*)

HISTORY AND DESCRIPTION OF THE COMMUNITY SERVICE
  WRITING PROJECT IN THE WRITING AND CRITICAL
  THINKING PROGRAM AT STANFORD UNIVERSITY
COMMUNITY SERVICE WRITING PROJECT: CURRENT
  AND FORMER SPONSORING AGENCIES
HAAS CENTER FOR PUBLIC SERVICE: AN INTRODUCTION
PRINCIPLES OF GOOD PRACTICE FOR COMBINING SERVICE
  AND LEARNING: From *Wingspread Journal*, published by
  The Johnson Foundation

HISTORY AND DESCRIPTION OF THE COMMUNITY SERVICE WRITING PROJECT IN THE WRITING AND CRITICAL THINKING PROGRAM AT STANFORD UNIVERSITY

In the fall of 1989, the Writing and Critical Thinking Program (formerly Freshmen English) launched an innovative pilot program in community service writing, in conjunction with the Haas Center for Public Service. (A description of
services provided by the Haas Center is provided later in this appendix.) The
community service writing project is designed to improve the academic writing
skills of first-year college students by incorporating writing for nonprofit
agencies into course work. Completion of a community service writing project
fulfills a portion of the university writing requirement in the Writing and
Critical Thinking Program.

Entering students have the option of taking a Writing and Critical Thinking
course that features a community service writing project. This year, 25 percent
of the courses have community service writing components. The academic
emphasis of the project is unique. Students receive academic credit for their
writing only. Our students work with agency personnel, their teachers, and
each other to produce writing projects ranging from newsletters, brochures,
and fact sheets to museum guides and grant proposals. Introduced early to
community service writing, many of our students go on to volunteer at community agencies; a number of these students have chosen a career direction
that grew out of their community service writing experiences. Although an
increasing number of universities all over the country are integrating service
learning and writing, our program is currently the only one to link service and
academic learning through writing projects in the first term of college.

We began the program with the idea of providing students in our classes
with a range of community service writing projects so that they could choose
a project that interested them. In the weeks before classes start, the placement
coordinator at the Haas Center works with agencies to develop a range of
research and writing projects. The placement coordinator distributes several
placements to each class. Once students decide which agency they want to
work for, they begin the process of contacting the agency supervisor and defining their writing tasks. Students work individually, in groups, with their

instructor in class, and during conferences to complete their writing. Students complete journals in which they record their agency meetings and reflections on their community service writing experiences, as well as their progress on writing assignments. When their projects are completed, the students write evaluations of their learning process for the Haas Center and the Writing and Critical Thinking Program. The instructor and agency receive copies of the completed writing projects.

In our first year, 100 students and eight agencies participated in the Community Service Writing Project. The program is now halfway into its fifth year, and more than 1000 students have worked on writing projects at approximately 100 service organizations. The program is evaluated quarterly by students, instructors, and agency personnel. These evaluations of the project indicate that students feel they benefited in the following ways:

- Students' library research skills developed as they pursued writing projects on legal, environmental, health, and educational issues.
- Students have developed organizational skills, as well as more concise and purposeful writing styles, through writing about issue-related topics for specific audiences in their communities.
- Students have learned to work and write collaboratively because projects are completed by groups of three or four students, or by students writing separately before joining their individual research units together.
- Students have improved their revision skills by developing a realistic understanding of how a public agency expects revision to be handled and by working with their collaborators to complete a writing project.
- Students' skills in writing and critical thinking have shown marked improvement in their journals and evaluations, as well as in the context of academic and intellectual issues presented in their writing courses.
- Students' motivation and ability to write well have increased because they have had a real public audience for whom to write and because they know that what they write will have a direct impact, that what they write will make a difference.
- Students have developed their cultural awareness and understanding of different ethnic, social, and economic groups in their communities.

Below is a list of representative types of community service writing projects that have been completed by our students:

- One pair of students working at Project Read compiled a brochure that described all of the tutoring programs available to children in East Palo Alto and surrounding communities.
- One student working for the Support Network for Battered Women wrote a series of articles on domestic violence, including a book review and an essay on rape on campus.
- Students working with SPOON, a campus organization that distributes surplus food from the dorms to homeless shelters in the community, wrote brochures, fact sheets, and newsletters for members of the community and for students and faculty on campus.

- Another student group, helping at the Baylands Conservation Center, wrote two sets of information sheets on wildlife and water life, one set for adults and one for children under the age of twelve.
- Two groups working for La Raza Central Legal, an immigration law agency for Hispanics, produced a newsletter, a history of the organization for a twenty-year-reunion fund-raising drive, and a grant proposal.

Agency representatives have reported almost unanimously that our writing students have fulfilled an important function by informing the community of their services and helping to effect change; agencies are now contacting us regularly to request student writers. They are satisfied that students are learning more about community issues, about how nonprofit organizations function, and about how research and writing are completed in real-world settings. Agencies are pleased that a number of students have continued to volunteer after completing their writing projects; students have continued to volunteer at agencies such as the Stanford Blood Bank, Reach Out, The Patient Resource Center at the Stanford Hospital, La Raza Central Legal, and Project Read.

COMMUNITY SERVICE WRITING PROJECT: CURRENT AND FORMER SPONSORING AGENCIES

Adolescent Counseling Services

Adult Independent Development Center

Amnesty International USA Refugee Office

Asian American Students Association (AASA)

Asian Americans for Community Involvement

Bay Area Action

Baylands Nature Interpretive Center

Body Image, Food, and Self-Esteem

Catholic Charities—Development Office

Catholic Charities—Immigration and Refugee Services

Central Committee for Conscientious Objectors

Child Advocacy Council of San Mateo and Santa Clara Counties

Citizens for a Better Environment

City of San Mateo

Committee for Green Foothills

Community Association for Retarded, Inc.

Consortium for Young Women

Disability Resource Center (DRC)

East Palo Alto Historical and Agricultural Society

Ecumenical Hunger Program

Ellipse

Environmental Volunteers

Families in Transition

Food First

Friends for Youth

Friends of Kauai

Girl Scouts of Santa Clara County

Global Exchange

Haas Center for Public Service

Health Education and Training Center

Health Improvement Program (HIP)

Health Promotion Program (HPP)

Hesperian Foundation

HomeBase

Hunger and Homeless Action Coalition of San Mateo County

Independent Living Resource Center

Keys School

La Raza Central Legal

Latino Leadership Opportunity Program (LLOP)

Los Lupenos de San Jose

Magic, Inc.

March of Dimes

Mayfield Community Clinic

Mid-Peninsula Citizens for Fair Housing

Mid-Peninsula YWCA Rape Crisis Center

Multicultural Training Resource Center

Open Shutter Productions

Overseas Development Network

Palo Alto Adolescent Services Corporation (PAASC)

Peninsula Center for Peace and Justice

Peninsula Conservation Center Foundation

Peninsula Humane Society

Planned Parenthood of Santa Clara County

Project Read, East Palo Alto

Project Read, Menlo Park

Project Read, Redwood City

Rainforest Action Network

Ravenswood-Stanford Tutoring Program

Reach Out (newsletter)

S.E.E.D.

SPCA Hearing Dog Program

SPOON

San Francisco Food Bank

San Francisco Museum of Modern Art

San Francisco School Volunteers—Community Studies and Service Program

San Francisco Zoo

San Mateo Battered Women's Services

San Mateo County Community Schools

Santa Clara Family Living Center

Service League of San Mateo County

Shanti

Shule Mandela Academy

Sierra Club International Committee

South Bay Sanctuary Covenant

Stanford Blood Center

Stanford Center for African Studies

Stanford-in-Government

Stanford Mid-Peninsula Urban Coalition

Stanford School of Engineering Pre-College Program

Students for Environmental Action at Stanford (SEAS)

Student Environmental Action Coalition (SEAC)

Support Network for Battered Women

Surviving! (newsletter)

TeleSensory Training Department (Linked to Open Shutter)

20%+ by 2020

Urban Ministry of Palo Alto

Volunteers in Asia

WATCH: Women and Their Children's Housing

Wildlife Rescue

The Wilderness Society

Women's Cancer Resource Center

Youth and Family Assistance

Youth Science Institute (newsletter)

HAAS CENTER FOR PUBLIC SERVICE: An Introduction

> To be literate as a citizen requires more than knowledge and information; it includes the exercise of personal responsibility, active participation, and personal commitment to a set of values.[1]

Established in 1985, the Haas Center for Public Service represents Stanford's institutional commitment to education for civic responsibility. By engaging students in the widest variety of service activities—through hands-on action, policy research, or community problem solving—the Center enriches their education and inspires them to commit their lives to improving society.

Through the Haas Center, more than 3000 students annually join staff, faculty, policy makers, and community members in local, national, and international voluntary efforts. The Center is home to varied student service organizations and University programs, among them a Public Service Opportunities Clearinghouse, the Stanford Volunteer Network, the Community Service Writing Project, the Ravenswood Stanford Tutoring Program, the East Palo Alto Stanford Summer Academy, and Reach Out. Through the Center's "study-service connections" initiative, staff work with faculty and students to connect service and study across the curriculum in forty different courses. In addition, the Center serves as the campus base for Stanford in Washington, an intensive academic program in the nation's capitol. The Center administers public service fellowship programs and sponsors the annual "You Can Make a Difference" Conference, which brings nationally known speakers to campus to address policy issues such as world hunger, the environment, education, and public health. The Center is guided by a Faculty Steering Committee chaired by Dr. Shirley Brice Heath, and a National Advisory Board chaired by Peter S. Carpenter.

The Haas Center has exceeded all expectations for success. Service has become part of student life in classrooms, in the residences, and in extra-curricular programs. According to recent senior surveys over 70 percent of undergraduates are involved in public service during their Stanford careers (up from 49 percent in 1984). Through partnerships which the Center has

---

[1]Richard L. Morrill, "Educating for Democratic Values." *Liberal Education.* Vol. 68, No. 4, 1982.

developed with local government agencies, the Ravenswood City School District in East Palo Alto, the Bay Area Homelessness Program, and numerous nonprofit organizations, more than 3000 students contribute over 70,000 volunteer hours annually each academic year.

The Haas Center is a magnet and training ground for Stanford's finest students—eight of ten recent Rhodes Scholarship recipients were actively engaged in the Center as were a majority of recent Marshall and Truman Scholars and winners of the Dean's Service, Dinkelspiel, and Sterling awards. Increasingly, incoming freshmen tell us that this public service program is an important factor in their decision to select Stanford over competing universities.

The Haas Center is recognized nationally as a model program, responsible for changes in both students and undergraduate education. In *each* of the past three years representatives from more than 100 colleges and universities have visited the Center to learn about our programs. During the summer of 1991 the Center hosted the Campus Compact Institute for Integrating Service with Academic Study, which brought teams of faculty from 15 colleges and universities to Stanford for a week of "service-learning" curriculum development.

In April 1993 the Haas Center opened a new 14,000-square-foot building. The new quarters allow us to house Volunteers in Asia and forty student and University service organizations, and enables us to develop a Public Service Fellows program for faculty and national leaders.

> [Stanford students] are saying—with exuberance—that we have a future. They have seen firsthand that they can make a difference. They have learned the habits of commitment to public purpose that will serve the nation well in the years ahead.[2]

For more information contact:

Timothy K. Stanton, Director
Haas Center for Public Service
P.O. Box 5848
Stanford, CA 94309-3473
(415) 723-0992

PRINCIPLES OF GOOD PRACTICE FOR COMBINING SERVICE AND LEARNING: From *Wingspread Journal*, published by The Johnson Foundation

The National Society for Experiential Education conducted consultations with over seventy organizations interested in service and learning. In May 1989 a small advisory group met at Wingspread to compose the preamble and language of the ten Principles. We have included below the preamble and key points of the Principles.

[2]John W. Gardner, "Centennial Challenge." Address given as part of Stanford Centennial Celebration, September 29, 1991.

Preamble

We are a nation founded upon active citizenship and participation in community life. We have always believed that individuals can and should serve.

It is crucial that service toward the common good be combined with reflective learning to assure that service programs of high quality can be created and sustained over time, and to help individuals appreciate how service can be a significant and ongoing part of life. Service, combined with learning, adds value to each and transforms both.

Those who serve and those who are served are thus able to develop the informed judgment, imagination, and skills that lead to a greater capacity to contribute to the common good.

The Principles that follow are a statement of what we believe and are essential components of good practice. We invite you to use them in the context of your particular needs and purposes.

1. An effective program engages people in responsible and challenging actions for the common good.
2. An effective program provides structured opportunities for people to reflect critically on their service experience.
3. An effective program articulates clear service and learning goals for everyone involved.
4. An effective program allows for those with needs to define those needs.
5. An effective program clarifies the responsibilities of each person and organization involved.
6. An effective program matches service providers and service needs through a process that recognizes changing circumstances.
7. An effective program expects genuine, active, and sustained organizational commitment.
8. An effective program includes training, supervision, monitoring, support, recognition, and evaluation to meet service and learning goals.
9. An effective program insures that the time commitment for service and learning is flexible, appropriate, and in the best interests of all involved.
10. An effective program is committed to program participation by and with diverse populations.